Owen County Kentucky

Stray Books 1 & 2

1819-1830

AND

1830-1864

Carrie Eldridge

Heritage Books
2024

HERITAGE BOOKS

AN IMPRINT OF HERITAGE BOOKS, INC.

Books, CDs, and more—Worldwide

For our listing of thousands of titles see our website
at
www.HeritageBooks.com

Published 2024 by
HERITAGE BOOKS, INC.
Publishing Division
5810 Ruatan Street
Berwyn Heights, MD 20740

Heritage Books by the author:

1860 Census, Cabell County, West Virginia

An Atlas of Appalachian Trails to the Ohio River

An Atlas of German Migration and America

An Atlas of Northern Trails Westward from New England

An Atlas of Settlement between the Appalachian Mountains and the Mississippi/Missouri Valleys: 1760–1880

An Atlas of the Southern Trails to the Mississippi

An Atlas of Trails West of the Mississippi River

Cabell County's Empire for Freedom

Cabell County, Virginia/West Virginia, Superior Court Records, 1843–1848

Etna Iron Works: Ledger Book - Expense Records, 1876–1878 (Final Ledger), Lawrence County, Ohio

Looking at the Personal Diaries of William F. Dusenberry of Bloomingdale, (Cabell County), Virginia/West Virginia, 1855 and 1856, Plus Parts of 1862, 1869, 1870, and 1871

Minute Books: Cabell County, [West] Virginia Minute Book 1, 1809–1815

Miscellaneous Cabell County, West Virginia Records: Order Book Overseers of the Poor, 1814–1861; Fee Book, 1826–1839; 1857–1859 (Rule Book); Cabell Land for Tax Purposes, 1861–1865

Nicholas County, Kentucky Property Tax Lists, 1800–1811 with Indexes to Deed Books A & B (2), and C

Nicholas County, Kentucky Records: Stray Book 1, 1805–1811; Stray Book 2, 1813–1819; Stray Book 3, 1820–1870; and Execution Book A, 1801–1878

On the Frontier of Virginia and North Carolina

Owen County, Kentucky Stray Books 1 & 2: 1819–1830, 1830–1864

Torn Apart: How Cabell Countians Fought the Civil War

International Standard Book Number
Paperbound: 978-0-7884-2001-6

AniMap County Boundary Map - KENTUCKY - 1788

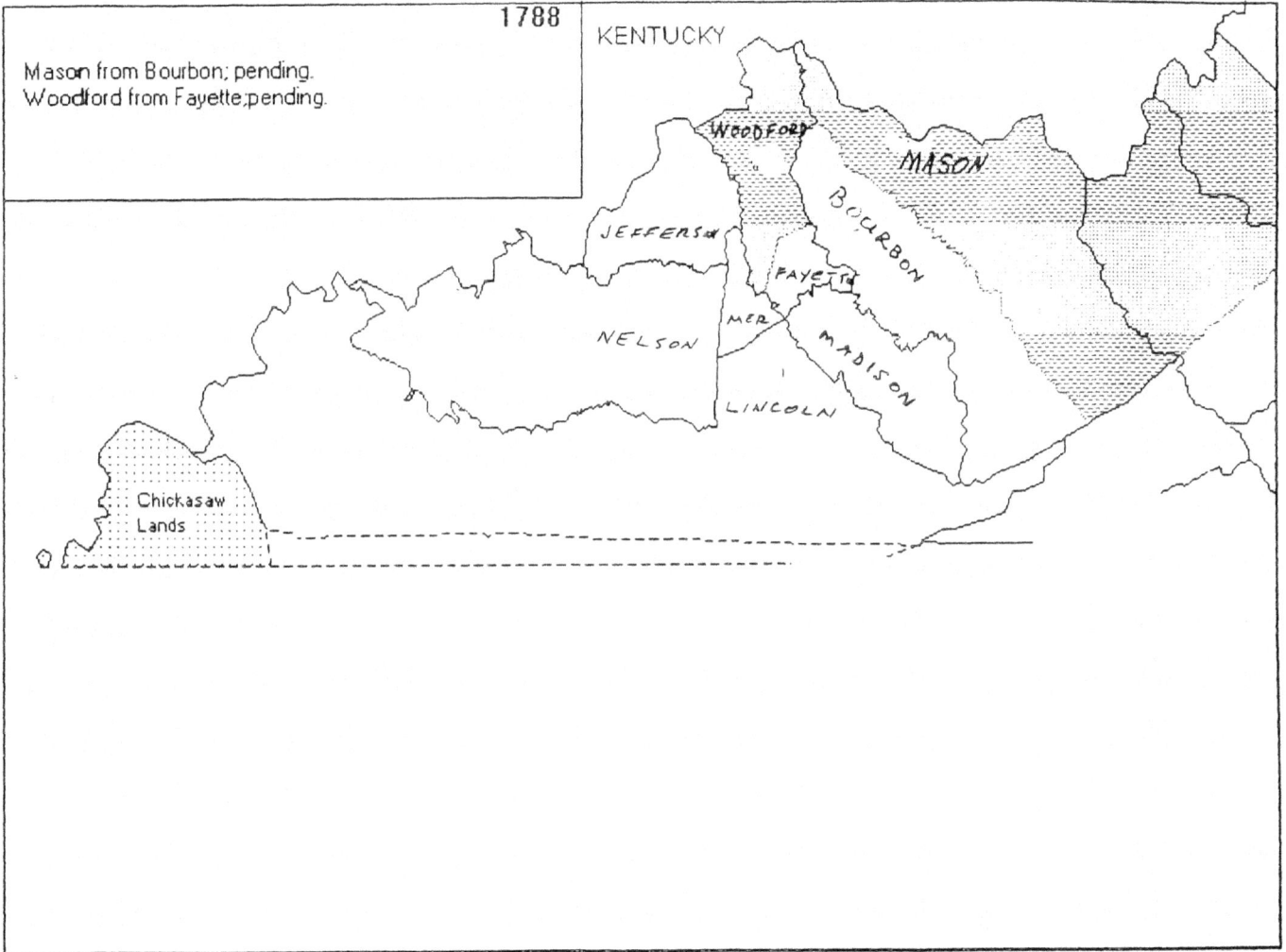

1788   KENTUCKY

Mason from Bourbon; pending.
Woodford from Fayette; pending.

WOODFORD   MASON

JEFFERSON   BOURBON

FAYETTE

NELSON   MER.   MADISON

LINCOLN

Chickasaw
Lands

STRAYS   BOOK

Here is a little known book that can be a real find when it still remains in the county. A STRAY BOOK is a listing of all the strayed animals that have been found and claimed before the Justice of the Peace.

These animals may have been let loose when their owners could not feed them, lost through high water or other natural disasters, separated from groups traveling through the area or simply lost.

The person who took the time to catch and corral the animals could have them appraised before the JP and then take them home, if no one claimed them the finder had new livestock.

These books are great because they tell not only the finders name, but also where the stock was taken; most often near the finders homestead. Here, is an excellent LOCATOR because most of the entries give a very good description where the livestock was found.

The entries also give some idea about the county itself. Owen County was a connector between the Kentucky Bluegrass and Cincinnati on the Ohio River. Apparently many animals were rafted down the Kentucky River and were lost along the Owen County stretch.

With the changes in transportation, Owen County is today isolated; but in the nineteenth century, it was on the main transporation route.

Because of the repetion of the animals description and markings, it was decided to delete that information from the abstracts. Anyone interested in early animal husbandry would find their descriptions of the animals quite informative.

Locations named in 1819-1830 Stray Book

Communities	Mills	Other man made sites
Owenton	Sander's New Mill	Million's Tavern
Heslerville	Sander's Old Mill	Razor's Ferry
Harrisburg	Sander's Upper Mill	Brinham's Post Office
Liberty	Herndon's Mill	Steel's Old Road
New Liberty	Spark's Horse Mill	McDowell's Trace
Marion	Vallandingham's Mill	Wm. Nelson's Tavern
Jonas Jones (?)	Wilhoite's Horse Mill	Emman's Meeting Pl.
Cobb's Station	Campbell's Mill	
Clay Lick Settlement	Kemper's Mill	
Hudson Settlement	Covover's Mill	
Baker's Settlement	Jacob Hunter's Mill	
	Fleming's Mill	
	Stafford Jones Mill	
	Branham's Mill	
	Jones Mill on Eagle	

Rivers and Creeks

Kentucky River	Cedar Creek	Eagle Creek
Land ripple of the Kentucky	Elm Lick of Cedar	Gaines Br.
Mountain Island	Indian Fork of Cedar	Little Lick
	Mathews Br. of Cedar	Big Lick of Eagle
	Blue Lick of Cedar	3 Forks of Eagle
	Sulphur Lick	Caney Fork
	North Fork	Quill's Branch
	Clark's Branch	Paine's Run
	Shortridge's Fork	Trace Fork
	Muscle Shoals	

Lavern or Savern Creek (never did decide which)

Elkhorn Creek	Drennan's Creek	Dickey's Lick Fork
6 Mile Creek	Brush Creek	Payne's Run
Mill Creek	Pond's Branch	Stevenson's Creek
Ray's Fork	Elk Creek	Richland Creek
Feat Creek	White Oak Lick	Levallon Fork
Indian Creek	Steven's Creek	Three Forks
Stephen's Creek	Bone Lick	
Sugar Camp Br.	Drennan's Creek	

Payne's Bottom	Steel's Old Road	Porter's Road
Thomas's Bottom	State Road	

hand writing
undecided---Sydnor- Lydnor   Quills - Guills-   Savern - Lavern

Owen County, Kentucky   Stray Book   1819-1830
(Owen County unless marked)

sorrel horse	Taken up by Colby Holbrooks living in Owen County near James Herdons Mill, one dark chestnut, some (mean) horse, 10 years old a small star in his forehead, a scar on his near hind foot just above his hoof, also a white spot on his near (arme) fourteen hands three inches high, a speck in his near eye appraised to $25 from me this 2nd day of June 1819. Wm.Cobbs JPOC
Bay horse	Taken up by John Winscott living in Owen County on Elk Creek, one bay horse four years old, a star in his forehead a small snip, three white feet, judged to be fourteen hands high appraised at $35 before me this 12th of June 1819 Wm.Cobb. JPOC
Sorrel mare	Taken by John Smith on Eagle Creek, a sorrel mare 5 years old & 14 hands with star branded on near bullock with B, had on small bell apprasied $35. 8 jun 1819 Jacob Hesler JPOC
Bay horse	Taken by James Frazier on Kentucky River opposite mouth of 6 Mile Ck Owen Co., bay horse 4 years old 15 hands with some white on his feet, a star and a snip, no brand appraised $100 20 may 1819 John Scrimsher
Dark sorrel horse	Taken by James Frazier on Kentucky River in bottom opposite mouth of 6 Mile Ck. Dark sorrel horse, 3 years old, 14 1/2 hands particular flesh mark, appraised $50, also bright sorrel mare 2 years old, some white on all her feet, small star & snip appraised $15 5 jun 1819 John Schrimsher
Bay horse	James Wymer on Hudson Settlement, Owens County, a Bay horse, four years old, about 14 hands high, no marks or brands presumeably, the hairs of his tail cut square off, appraised to $20 6 jun 1819 John Scrimsher
Dark roan horse	Taken by Colby Holbrook, Owen County near James Herndon's Mill, one dark roan horse, five years old, 14 1/2 hands high, a blemish in his mane, appraise $47.50 5 Jul 1819 Wm. Cobb
Two sheep	Taken by James Warwick ,two miles from James Herndon's Mill, two stray sheep, one weather marked with a wallow fork in the right ear, an ewe no marked, appraised to $150 each 1 apr 1819 Wm.Cobb JP
Bay mare	Taken by Charles Williams at Williamsburg bay mare 7 years old about 14 hands 3 inches, a blaze face, both hind feet white, some white near fore foot, shod before, no brand, appraised $52.50, also bay yearling man colt with blaze face, both hind feet white,

some white near fore foot, midling short tail no brand appraised $12   20 apr 1819   John Scrimsher

dark bay mare Taken by Daniel (Lett) on 3 Forks of Eagle Ck, one dark bay mare small star in forehead, blind right eye about 12 years old, appraised $25 27 apr 1819 Wm.Cobb

sorrel horse Taken by John Cobb two strays, one sorrel horse 4 years old, small star forehead 14 1/2 hands appraised $45, black filly 3 years old, star & snip, 2 hind feet white 13 1/2 hands appraised $25 7 may 1819   Wm.Cobb JP

bay horse Taken by James Frazier on Kentucky River opposite mouth of 6 Mile Ck, one bay horse 4 years old, 15 hands 3 inches, some white on all feet star and snip, no brand appraised $100 20 may 1819 John Scrimsher

bay horse Taken by Charles Tyler on Kentucky River below mouth of Elkhorn, bay horse 14 to 15 years old, 14 hands 3 inches, star in forehead, both hind feet white, saddle spots on back no brand also, bay stud colt 2 years old, star in forehead inclining to right, both hind feet white, hair of tail cropped square apprised $25 14 jul 1819 John Scrimsher

bay mare Taken by (Silas) B.Colvert waters of Cedar Ck near Sulphur Lick bay mare 8 to 9 years old, 14 1/2 hands , star on forehead, snip on nose, both hind feet white no brand appraised $30 3 aug 1819

bay mare Taken by George Vallandingham on State Road Owen Co. bay mare 14 hands, 7 years old with star & snip, both hind feet white and blind left eye appraised $35 21 aug 1819 Jacob Hiser

black horse Taken by William Woodside at mouth of (Lavern) Ck, black horse 7 years old 13 hands, both hind feet white branded IK appraised $25 26 jun 1819 John Glass JP

black mare Taken by Benjamin Robinson near Rains Bottom one black mare 4 years old small star on forehead 13 hands, near hind foot and off fore foot white, branded with pot hook on near shoulder appraised $15   1 nov 1819 Wm. Cobb JPOC

sorrel mare Taken by William Curry near Sulphur Lick of Cedar Ck, sorrel mare 3 years old 14 hands, star on forehead & snip on nose, both hind feet white no brand appr $35 1 nov 1819 John Scrimsher

bay mare Taken by Thomas Carter in Clay Lick Settlement Owen County bright bay mare two years old no natural marks, branded on the near shoulder with one pin stripe, appraised to $17.50 7 sep 1819 John Scrimsher

(ALL STRAY ENTRIES SIMILAR TO ABOVE)

White cow Rone — Taken by William Curry at Sulphur Lick on Cedar Creek Owen County appraised $18, also "veal team" yearling appraised to $4 1 dec 1819 John Scrimsher

Bred Cow — Taken by Harman Hawkins on Cedar Creek Owen County one mile from Sulphur Lick, bred cow 9 pr 10 years old. appraised to $13, 14 dec 1819   John Scrimsher

Bred Heifer — Taken by Benjamin Hawkins on Cedar Creek Owen County one mile from Sulphur Lick, bred Heifer 2 years old, appraised to $6 1 dec 1819 John Scrimsher

(Red) Steer — Taken by William R Smoot on Mill Creek Owen County 2 miles from Clay Lick, appraised to $4 - 7 dec 1819 John Scrimsher

Bull — Taken by John Bowan in Owen County on the waters of (Savem) Creek, a bull appraised $6.50 December 23,1819 Jacob Hesler

Bay Mare — Taken by Robert G. True living on main Eagle Creek Owen County bay mare appraised $25.00 March 21, 1820 John Glass

Sorrel Mare — Taken by John Vallendingham Owen County on Steals old road two miles above Michael Murrays, sorrel mare appraised $50 April 29, 1820 Thomas L. Bryan

Sorrell Mare — Taken by William Suiter living on Steals old road four mile above Harris Burgh appraised $12 15 April 1820 Thomas L. Bryan

Sorrell Horse — Taken by Colby Holbrooks living near James Herndon's Mill Owen County appraised $25 2nd June 1819 Wm.Cobb JPOC

Bay Mare — Taken by John Willis livings on Rays Fork 1 1/2 mile from Wm. Nelson's tavern Owen County. Appraised $35 11 dec 1819 John Glass JPOC

Sorrell Colt — Taken by Belfield Glass living on Caney fork of Eagle Creek, Owen County appraised $8.00 23rd December 1819 John Glass JPOC

Sorrell Mare — Taken by William Curns at the Sulphur Lick on Cedar Creek Owen County appraised $35 1st December 1819 John Scrimsher

Bay Mare — Taken by Thomas Carter in Clay Lick Settlement Owen County appraised $17.50 7th September 1819 John Scrimsher

White Cow — Taken by William Curry at the Sulphur Lick Cedar Creek appraised $4.00 1st December 1819 John Scrimsher

Red Heifer — Taken by Silas B. Calvert on Cedar Creek Owen County 2 1/2 miles from Sulphur Lick 1st December 1819 John Scrimsher

Bay Mare — Taken by George Vallandingham on Steals old road bay mare appraised by $35 21st August 1819 Jacob Hesler JPOC

White Steer — Taken by Alexander Guthrey on the waters of Savern Creek and Cedar Creek appraised $5 December 1, 1819 Jacob Hesler

Red Heifer — Taken by Charles Tyler on Kentucky River below mouth Elkhorn Owen County appraised $2.50 27th March 1820 John Scrimsher

Brown Mare — Taken by Lewis Wilhoit at the cross roads on Savern Creek 3 1/2 miles from Williamsburgh Owen County. Appraised $30 29th April 1829 John Scrimsher

Sorrell Mare — Taken by George Vallandingham on Steels old Road 2 mile above Michael Murray's appraised $50 29th April 1820 Thos.L.Bryan

Sorrell Mare — Taken by John Williams near Williamsburgh, Owen County appraised $15 - May 1820 John Scrimsher

Sorrell Horse — Taken by Paul Faught on Kentucky River opposite mouth of Feat Creek appraised $55. 10th June 1820 John Scrimsher

Bay Mare — Taken by Robert Hadden on water of the Twinns appraised $30 31th May 1820 Thomas L. Bryan

Black White Hog — Taken by John Wimore on Stephen's Creek, 2 years old appraised $4.50 10th 1820 Jacob Hesler

D.Bay Horse — Taken by Cain Spicer on North Fork of Cedar Creek one mile up, appraised $25 - 2oth June 1820 John Scrimsher

Red Cow — Taken by Rhodes Dehoney on McDowell old Trace of Indian Creek appraised $9 17th December 1819 John Scrimsher

Brown Mare — Taken by Tobias Wilhoit on waters of Savern & Cedar Creeks apprasied $50 19th June 1820 Jacob Hesler

Brown Mare — Taken by Thomas Jones near Stafford Jones Mill Owen County appraised $20 1st July 1820   John Glass JPOC

Gray Horse — Taken by Richard Williams 1/2 mile from Wiliamsburg appraised $20   7th September 1820 John Scrimsher

Bay Horse — Taken by Charles Williams at Williamsburg apprasied $40 27th September 1820 John Scrimsher

Red Heifer — Taken by John Scrimsher on Cedar Creek 4 1/2 miles from

Black   Williamsburg, bull has bar and slit brand 13t November
Speckled bull   1820 Thos. L. Bryant

D Roan   Taken by Charles Williams at Williamsburg, horse appraised
Horse $45. mare apprasied $35 4th November 1820 John Scrimsher
R R Mare Justice Peace Owen County

Brindle   Taken by Colly Shipp on the road leading from mouth of Savern
Steer   to Heslerville appraised $7.50 15 November 1820 Jn.Scrimsher

Brindle   Taken by Harmon Hawkins on the road from Georgetown to
Steer'   Branhams post office on Cedar Creek appraised $4 19 Dec 1820

Nine   Taken by John Glass on Steels Road near Heslersville, two sandy
Hogs   barrows, four white hogs and three spotted ones and two
             unmarked shoats appraised $13 NB one white one is sow
             29th November 1820 John Glass

Brindle Taken by Belfield Glass on Cany Fork branch of Eagles Creek
Bull   23 September 1820   John Glass JPOC

Brindle Taken by Zacheriah Woolem living near Campbells Mill appraised
Steer $4 18th day November 1820

Bay   Taken by John Glass living near Heslersville appraised $8
Mare   23rd November 1820 John Glass JPOC

Black   Taken by Alexander Guthery on waters of Cedar Creek
Steer   12th December 1820 Jacob Hesler

Work   Taken by Isaac Hadden on waters of Stephen's Creek appraised
Steer $12 10 December 1820 Jacob Hesler

Red Speckled Taken by Samuel Sanders near Branham's Mill appraised
Steer $7. 20th November 1820   John Scrimsher

Black   Taken by William Curry at the Sulphur Lick of Cedar Creek
Heifer   appraised $3.50 plus red yearling $3 1st December 1820
             John Schrimsher

Piped   Taken by William Thomas near Kentucky River four miles above
             mouth of Drennan Creek appraised $3.50 1 December 1820

Red & White Taken by Lewis Wilhite on Savern Creek. Appraised $8
Steer   13 September 1820 Jacob Hesler

Black   Taken by George Razer four mile above mouth of Drennens Ck
Stear   on Kentucky River   4th nov 1820 E.D.George JPOC

Eleven Hogs	Taken by John W. Holladay on Sugar Camp Branch of Stephens Ck 6 nov 1820 Wm.Cobb JPOC
Black Mare	Taken by Abraham McMeens on Laren Creek 3 jul 1821 Jacob Hesler
Brindle Stear	Taken by Andrew McMeens on Laren Creek yearling appraised $4 3 jan 1821 Ja. Hesler
Red Steer	Taken by Andrew Baker on Twinn Ck yearling appraised $3.25 Ja. Hesler
Pided Steer	Taken by Caleb Squires on Brush Creek appraised $11 15 nov 1820 Thos. L. Bryan JPOC
R & W Steer	Taken by Robert Sanders in Gallatine County near New Liberty 10 feb 1821 Reuben Adams JPOC
R & W Heifer	Taken by (Jerd) Perkins on Elk Creek near Cobbs Station also red & white steer & black steer 27 jan 1827 Jas.Herndon
Brindle Cow	Taken by Robert Jones Owen Co. near Henry Sparks horse mill apprasied $10 10 feb 1821 John Scrimsher
Red Steer	Taken by James Gess eight miles from Heslersville on Eagle Creek 13 jan 1821 Thos. L. Bryan JPOC
pale red heifer	Taken by Sherwood Maddox one mile from Harrisburg on Twinns Ck. apprasied $1.25 20 jan 1821 Thos.L.Bryan
sorrell mare	Taken by Amos Clark on Savern Creek appraised $40 12 mar 1821 Jacob Hesler
Black Cow	Taken by Joel Bontton on the Twinns 1/2 mile from Harrisburg 19 feb 1821 Thos.L.Bryan
Bay Mare	Taken by Francis Goddard on Cany Fork of Eagle Creek 24 apr 1821 John Glass JPOC
sorrel horse	Taken by George Marshall on Quills Branch of Eagle Creek 8 may 1821 John Glass JPOC
ram 4 sheep	Taken by Richard Osburn near Cobs Station 18 apr 1821 Jas. Herndon JPOC
r & w bull	Taken by John Moore on waters of Brush Creek 1 1/2 mile from Harrisburg 30 mar 1821 Thos.L.Bryan JPOC

Dam Mare	Taken by Benjamin Stephens on Kentucky River above mouth of Cedar 2 jun 1821 Peter Sanders JPOC
sorrel mare +	Mare, horse & colt taken by Perry Thornton on Clarks Branch of Cedar (living on George Hardin's land) 2 jul 1821 P.Sanders
Steer	Taken by Minos Ratcliff living on the long line of the County $4 13 jan 1821 Wm.Cobb JPOC
D.Brown Horse	Taken by Captain John Smith near Cobb's old station, 14 jun 1821 Jas.Herndon JPOC
Black Horse	Taken by Jacob Rasier on waters of Mill Creek five miles from mouth of Clay's Lick 27 jun 1821 Thos.L.Bryan
Bay Mare	Taken by Ellis Fitzjeral (by the liberty of Wilford Stephens) living on Stephen's land on Clark's Branch of Cedar Creek 2 march 1821 Peter Sanders JPOC
Sorrel Mare	Taken by Samuel (Culd) in (Heslerville) 6th aug 1821 John Glass JPOC

(next several pages badly water damaged)

Brindle Cow	Taken by Asa Colt at Muscle Shoals (Water damage) 19th November 1821 Wm.Cobb JOPC
?	Taken by Robert Southwith near Heslerville ? nov 1821 John Glass JPOC
?	Taken by John Bowen Owen County ? 17th Nov 1821 Jacob Hesler JPOC
R & W Heifer	Taken by Cain Spicer living on Shortridge's Fork of Cedar Creek 19 Nov 1821 Peter Sanders JPOC
Brindle cow-Steer	Taken by Tobias Wilhite on the ridge between Cedar & Laverns creeks 21 nov 1821 Peter Sanders JPOC
2 brindle heifers	Taken by William Clark at the (Blue) Lick of Cedar ? Nov 1821 Peter Sanders
Red Steer	Taken by John Batts at Clay Lick flat (?) 6 dec 1821 Peter Sanders JPOC
two Heifers	Taken by Judah Parrish Owen County ?? Benj.Holliday JPOC

pg 25

Brindle	Taken by Hugh Shelton on waters of Big Twin
Steer	26 nov 1821 Ben.Holliday

White Ram — Taken by John Smith, post rider, near the mountain island
appraised $1.50   1 dec 1821   James Herndon JPOC

Brindle Steer — Taken by Thomas Arnold on Big Twin Branch near Marion's
?   1821   Moses Baker JPOC

Red Steer — Taken by Moses Baker Jr. on Little Twin about three miles
from Marion   23 nov 1821   Moses Baker JPOC

White Sow Spotted Barrow — Taken by Michael Murray in Owen County near the Center
apprasied $2.50 ???
also appraised $2.50 ???
8th dec 1821   Jacob Hesler

Black Steer — Taken by David Maddox on Twin Creek two miles from
Harrisburg   ?? 1821   Thos. L. Bryan JPOC

Muley Steer — Taken by Jeremiah Harrison on Stephenson Creek
Dec 1821   Thos. L. Bryan JPOC

Sorrell Mare — Taken by Charles Williams at Williamsburg
19th - 1821   Peter Sanders

Bay Horse — Taken by James Hardin on Cedar Creek
24 oct 1821   Peter Sanders JPOC

Sorrell Horse — Taken by Joseph Runyon on Stevesons Creek
11 aug 1821   Jacob Hesler JPOC

Red Heifer — Taken by Job Garvey near Jonas Jones appraised $1.75
27 dec 1821   Reuben Adams JPOC

Boar — Taken by James Reeds living near Jonas Jones
27 dec 1821   Reuben Adams JPOC

Hog — Taken by Job Garvey(Ganey) near Jonas Jones
27 dec 1821   Reuben Adams

Red Heifer — Taken by James Stewart near Harrisburg
appraised $3.00 10 jan 1822   Reuben Adams JPOC

D.Red Heifer — Taken by Robert Smither on Pond Branch
17 dec 1821   Peter Sanders JPOC

Cow etc.	Taken by William Curry at the Sulphur Lick on Cedar Creek, Red Cow, White Heifer, Black Bull, White Muley Bull, Red Heifer total appraisal $25 16 dec 1821 Peter Sanders
B & W Stear	Taken by Augustus Burns on the Kentucky River near Henry Spark's Horse Mill 15 dec 1821 Peter Sanders
Red Cow	Taken by William Rowlett on Kentucky River mouth of Lavern Creek 5 jan 1822 Peter Sanders
cow etc.	Taken by Jonathan Stamper near mouth of Elk Creek, 4 head of cattle and a red and white pided stear 11 dec 1821 Wm.Cobb
ewe 3 lambs	Taken by James Vallandingham on Steels Road $1 each 25 dec 1821 Jacob Hesler
R & W Stear	Taken by Robert Hadden on Steels Road 30 dec 1821 Jacob Hesler
Red Stear	Taken by John Squires 2 mile from Harrisburg 12 jan 1822 Thos.L.Bryan
B & W Heifer	Taken by William Bowen on Lavern Creek five miles from Owenton on the Frankfort Road 17 jan 1822 Thos.L.Bryan
Bull	Taken by William McGee on Little Twin three miles from the mouth of Clay Lick 26 dec 1821 Thos.L.Bryan
R & W Stear	Taken by Abraham McMeens on north fork of Lavern Creek four miles from the mouth of Clay Lick 24 dec 1821 Thos.L.Bryan
Black Heifer	Taken by Ellis Fitzgerald on Clarks Branch of Cedar Creek 18 jan 1822 Peter Sanders JPOC
Heifer Bull	Taken by Robert Sanders at the crossing on Eagle's Creek leading from Frederick's (Creek) to Jonas Jones 4 jan 1822 Benj. Holliday JPOC
R & W Heifer	Taken by Robert Jones on Kentucky River near Spark's Horse Mill 25 feb 1822 Peter Sanders
Dun mouth Stear	Taken by Absolom Ivy on Big Twin, three to four miles from 12 jan 1822 Moses Baker JPOC
Red Stear	Taken by Isaac Haddon one and a half miles from Owenton 25 feb 1822 Thos.L.Bryan

Pided
Stear   Taken by Edward George on Kentucky River near mouth of
               (Lavern) Creek 11 mar 1822   Reuben Adams JPOC

Bay
Horse   Taken by James Herndon appraised $100
                26 sep 1822 Wm.Cobb

Heifer   Taken by Catherine Winscott on Mill Creek seven miles from
               Owenton   11 nov 1822   Thos.L.Bryan

Male
Hog   Taken by John Haddon on Eagle Creek three and one half miles
               from Owenton   23 nov 1822 Thos.L.Bryan

Gray
Horse   Taken by Celus B.Colvert on Clarkes Branch of Cedar Creek
               3 sep 1822   Peter Sanders

Bay
Horse   Taken by Charles Williams in Williamsburg 2 nov 1822
               Peter Sanders

White
Heifer   Taken by Daniel Shelton near New Liberty 6 nov 1822
               Reuben Adams

Sow   Taken by Thomas Brumley near New Liberty
6 shoats 30 nov 1822   Reuben Adams

Black
Stear   Taken by Lewis Ayers near New Liberty 2 stears appraised $11.50
               7 dec 1822   Reuben Adams JPOC

3   Taken by Caless Jones near New Liberty 7 dec 1822
Hogs   Reuben Adams

Bull   Taken by Alexander Jackson near Sanders Old Mill
               7 dec 1822   Reuben Adams

B & W Taken by Benjamin Robinson at Muscle Shoals of Eagle Creek
Heifer   19 nov 1822   Wm.Cobb

Pided   Taken by William Cobb on Eagle Creek
Bull   11 nov 1822   Jas. Hearndon JPOC

R & W Taken by Jonas Jones about 4 miles from New Liberty
Bull   4 nov 1822 Moses Baker

White   Taken by Benjamin Davis on Big Twin near Emans meeting
Barrow   place 23 nov 1822   Moses Baker

Stear   Taken by James Wamack by Eagle Creek   7 dec 1822
Bull   one appraised $5, the other $2.50   Jas. Hearndon

Bull   Taken by Daniel Lett on Three Forks 3 head of cattle and one
2 stears   bull $4 each   2nd Dec 1822   Wm.Cobb JPOC

White   Taken by John Reading on Indian Fork of Cedar Creek
Stear & Heifer   each appraised $8   27 nov 1822

Muly   Taken by Lewis Hardin on Cedar Creek   5th dec 1822
Heifer

R & W   Taken by Benjamin Hawkins on Cedar Creek   5 dec 1822
Heifer   Peter Sanders JPOC

Two   Taken by John Marqueson on the Kentucky River near the
Boats   mouth of the Twins One boat 62 ft long by ten wide, one small
            ferry 25 feet long   12 dec 1822   Moses Baker JPOC

Brindle   Taken by George Wyant near Sanders old mills, 12 dec 1822
Cow & calf

Red   Taken by Beverly Ballard on Indian Fork of Cedar Creek
Bull   14 dec 1822

Cow &   Taken by William Earsters on Elm Lick Fork of Cedar Creek
Calf   14 dec 1822

R & W   Taken by Martin Bramblete on Elm Lick of Cedar Creek
Heifer   14 dec 1822

R & W   Taken by Andrew Rogers on Cedar Creek at mouth of Smalls
Heifer   Branch   28 dec 1822

Five   Taken by Cain Spicer on Shortridge's Fork of Cedar Creek
Sheep   5 sheep, ram & ram lamb 31 dec 1822

Red   Taken by William Curry at the Sulphur Lick on Cedar Creek
Bull   7 jan 1823   Peter Sanders

R & W   Taken by John Swigert near New Liberty   18 dec 1822
Cow   Reuben Adams

Black   Taken by William Haddon on Stevenses Creek one and a half
heifer   miles from Owenton   3 jan 1823   Thos.L.Bryan

R & W   Taken by William Runyon in town of Owenton 24 dec 1822
heifer   Thos. L. Bryan

Black   Taken by William Suiter on waters of Twin Creek one quarter
Barrow   mile from Owenton   4 dec 1822 Thos.L. Bryan

R & W   Taken by Jacob Hesler near Owenton
Bull   10 dec 1822 Thos.L.Bryan

Red   Taken by Lewis Harden on Cedar Creek above (Brinbams) Mill
Stear   13 Jan 1823   Peter Sanders

R & W   Taken by Ennis Hardin above mouth of Cedar Creek two and
Stear   one half miles 24 jan 1823

Locust   Taken by Ennis Hardin on Kentucky River two and one half
Posts   miles above the mouth of Cedar Creek, two hundred posts
          appraised $10   24 jan 1823   Peter Sanders

Red   Taken by John L. Burchfield near the mountain island
Stear   19 jan 1823   Jas.Herndon

R & W   Taken by William Gaines on Dickey's Lick Fork
heifer   22 dec 1823 Jas.Herndon

B & W   Taken by John Perkins near Cobbs Station 27 dec 1822
Stear   Jas. Herndon

Heifer   Taken by Polly Sneed on head of Two Mile 25 jan 1823
Stear   Benj. Holliday JPOC

Black   Taken by Phillip Callendas on waters Twin Creek near Kemper's
Stear   Mill 28 dec 1822   Benj. Holliday

Red   Taken by Jacob Heam at Harrisburg, Owen County
Bull   17 dec 1822 Thos. L. Bryan

Red   Taken by George P. Thornton on Clark's Branch of Cedar Creek
Heifer   4 mar 1823   Peter Sanders

Red   Taken by James Herndon
Bull   17 dec 1822   Wm.Cobb

Sorrell   Taken by John W.Holliday   6 may 1823
Mare   Wm.Cobb JPOC

Yellow   Taken by William Massie on Payne's Run, yellow bay mare
Mare   25 apr 1823   James Herndon

Chestnut Taken by Jonas Jones on road leading from Cincinnati to New
Mare   Liberty apprasised $57.50   Benj. Holliday

Gray   Taken by Jesse Stamper on waters of Stevenson Creek 3 1/2 mile
Mare   from Owenton 5 may 1823   Thos.L.Bryan

Sorrell Horse	Taken by Michael Murray 3/4 mile from Owenton 25 aug 1823 Thomas L. Bryan
Bay Mare	Taken by Susannah O'Banion at Cobb's Station 2 oct 1823 William Cobb
2 Red Yearling	Taken by John Snell one mile from Owenton 6th dec 1823 Thos. L. Bryan
Red Cow	Taken by James Herndon at the Mountain Island 17 nov 1823 Wm. Cobb
Brindle Cow	Taken by David Shelton on Lavern Creek 5 dec 1823 Cyrus Wingate JPOC
Sorrell Colt	Taken by Elizabeth Black on Elm Lick of Cedar Creek 8 nov 1823 Peter Sanders
Muley Heifer	Martin Bramblett on Elm Lick Fork of Cedar Creek 8 nov 1823 Peter Sanders
Red Cow Calf	Taken by John Redding on Indian Fork of Cedar Creek 11 nov 1823 Peter Sanders
R & W Cow	Taken by David Hoover at Fleming Mill of Indian Creek 12 nov 1823 Peter Sanders
Pided Heifer	Taken by Celius B. Colvert on Cedar Creek near Sulphur Lick 19 nov 1823 Peter Sanders
Gray Mare	Taken by John Redding on Indian Fork of Cedar Creek 9 dec 1823 Peter Sanders
R & W Stear	Taken by Alexander Williams near Williamsburg 19 dec 1823 Peter Sanders
Red Heifer	Taken by William (Suiter) near Owenton 27 dec 1823 Thos. L. Bryan
B & W Boar	Taken by Lewis Neal on the road from Marion to Liberty 10 dec 1823 Moses Baker JPOC
a Sheep	Taken by Jacob Hesler near Owenton 21 jan 1824 Thos. L. Bryan
Wood Boat	Taken by Ennis Hardin near the land ripple on Kentucky River 54 feet, a cords wood, spade and spike 4 feb 1824 Peter Sanders

R & W   Taken by Thomas McKinsey near head waters of Twin
Stear   16 dec 1823 Benj. Holliday

Red   Taken by Moses Baker on the Twinn
Stear   20 dec 1823 Benj.Holliday

Black   Taken by John Brown on road from Frankfort to Owenton
Stear   five miles from Owenton appraised for a $6 note on the
             Bank of the Commonwealth 9 feb 1824 Cyrus Wingate

R & W   Taken by George Winder on Eagle Creek 3-4 miles from
Heifer   New Liberty 21 feb 1824 Moses Baker

Brindle   Taken by Aaron McDaniel near Marion
Stear   12 mar 1824 Moses Baker

R & W   Taken by Joseph George on Kentucky River one mile from
Stear   mouth of Drennons Creek 9 march 1824 E.D.George JPOC

Red   Taken by James Frazier on Kentucky River two miles above
Cow   Walter Ware house 12 feb 1824 E.D.George

Heifer   Taken by William Blanton on Two Mile   27 mar 1824
             Benj. Holliday

R & W   Taken by Sally Lewis on Paine's Run branch of Eagle Creek
Heifer   23 jan 1824   John Glass JPOC

Brindle   Taken by Richard L. Spanon on Paynes run branch of Eagle
Stear   Creek   20 dec 1823   John Glass

R & W   Taken by Zachariah Wollams near James Herndon's Mill
Stear   20 dec 1823   John Glass
p50
Bay   Taken by Beverly Ballard on Indian Fork of Cedar Creek
Mare   21 apr 1824 Peter Sanders

Black   Taken by Richard (Selre) 1 1/2 mile from Samuel Coburn's on
Mare   Richland Creek 20 may 1824   Thos.L. Bryan

Bay   Taken by Charles Williams in Williamsburg
Mare   31 may 1824   Peter Sanders

Chestnut   Taken by Zachariah Woollam near James Herndon's Mill
Horse   31 may 1824 Jas.Herndon

Bay   Taken by Andrew Rogers on Cedar Creek near the Sulphur Lick
Mare   23 oct 1824   Peter Sanders

Sandy Sow	Taken by (Ivy) Southworth and 4 shoats 10 oct 1824 Jas.Herndon
Sandy Sow	Taken by James Maddox on Brush Creek 1 nov 1824 Moses Baker
Bay	Taken by Elijah Martin on Eagle Creek 21 sep 1824 Wm. Cobb
Brindle Heifer	Taken by Ray Sidebottom 8 nov 1824 Benj. Holliday
Black Cow	Taken by Joshua (Spriers) on Kentucky River near mouth of Cedar Creek (also Pided muley stear and red muley heifer) appraised in Commonwealth money 1 nov 1824
R & W Heifer	Taken by Phillip Yancey 4 1/2 miles from Owenton on state road leading to New Liberty Benj. Holliday
R & W Stear	Taken by Oratio Gromm 4 miles from Owenton on the state road leading to New Liberty Benj.Holliday
R & W Heifer	Taken by David Clyton Wm.Cobb
Red Bull Calf	Taken by Willis Chandler at Payne's Bottom 13 nov 1824 Wm. Cobb
Nine Hogs	Taken by John Arnold on road leading from Marion to Liberty 29 nov 1824 Moses Baker
White Heifer	Taken by Sarah McDaniel on Kentucky River near Marion 6 dec 1824 Moses Baker
four Hogs	Taken by Alexander Williams on (Pon) Branch near mouth of Cedar 16 nov 1824
B & W Boar	Taken by Johnson Ballard on Kentucky River near mouth of Cedar 6 dec 1824
Red Heifer	Taken by Elijah (Canay) on Porter's Road between Shortridge's fork and Cedar's 10 dec 1824
Bay Mare	Taken by James Roberts on Sulphur Branch of Cedar Creek 10 dec 1824 Peter Sanders
Bay Horse	Taken by Augustine Smith near Conover's Mill on Eagle Creek 11 nov 1824 Reuben Adams

Brindle Heifer Taken by James Reeds near Jonas Jones
20 nov 1824   Reuben Adams

Black Cow Taken by Jeremiah Garvey near Jonas Jones
30 nov 1824   Reuben Adams

Pided Cow Taken by Charles Kemper on Twinn Creek
25 nov 1824   Reuben Adams

Three Ewes Taken by Thomas Rolands in Bakers Settlement
27 nov 1824   Reuben Adams

Spotted Hog Taken by Jacob --- near Owenton
8 nov 1824   Thos. L. Bryan

Red Hog Taken by William (Hnchell-Phiechell) two mile from
Owenton 11 nov 1824 Thos.L.Bryan

Yearling Taken by James Gess on waters of Stevenes Creek
13 dec 1824   Thos. L. Bryan

White Hog Taken by John Meek on the Twinn
Thos.L.Bryan

Pided Heifer Taken by Michael Murray near Owenton
1 dec 1824   R.Adams

Pided Stear Taken by Joseph Jones near Harrisburg
16 dec 1824 R.Adams

Pided Heifer Taken by Benjamin Marstler near New Liberty
18 dec 1824 R.Adams

One Hog ? Taken by John Snell one mile from Owenton
29 dec 1824 Thos.L.Bryan

Sorrell Mare Taken by Zachariah Williams on main Eagle Creek near
Herndon's Mill   29 jul 1824   John Glass

B & W Sow Taken by David Shelton in Owen County
18 dec 1824   Ben Holliday

R & W Heifer Taken by Celus B. Colvert near Sulphur Lick on Cedar
18 dec 1824 Peter Sanders

Brindle Heifer Taken by James Sanders at Little Lick of Eagle Creek
Ben Holliday 9 jan 1825

Pided Heifer	Taken by Robert Scott with levallon fork in left ear 27 dec 1824 27 dec 1824 Reuben Adams
Pied Heifer	Taken by Joel (Bontton) at Harrisburg 28 dec 1824 Reuben Adams
Brindle Heifer	Taken by Presly Hampton near Jonas Jones 11 jan 1825 Reuben Adams
Red Stear	Taken by Robert Sanders near Conover's Mill on Eagle Creek 11 jan 1825 Reuben Adams
White Stear	Taken by Robert Sanders on Eagle's Creek 11 jan 1825 Reuben Adams
Pied Heifer	Taken by Peyton R. Jennings near big lick on Eagle Creek 12 jan 1825 Reuben Adams
6 shoats	Taken by Robert Sanders on Eagle Creek near Conover's Mill 15 jan 1825 Reuben Adams
spotted Sow	Taken by Jonathan Kemper near New Liberty 2 jan 1825 Reuben Adams
Stear	Taken by James Sanders on Eagle Creek near the little lick 22 jan 1825 Benj. Holliday
Black Horse	Taken by Francis McComas living at Cobb's Station 10 feb 1825 William Cobb JPOC

(new clerk)

7 Hogs	Taken by Colby Holbrook of Owen County 5 feb 1825 Wm.Cobb
Brindle Heifer	Taken by Jesse Baker half way between New Liberty and Emman meeting house on Little Twin mar 1825 Moses Baker
Red Bull	Taken by John Jennings on Eagle Creek 5 mar 1825 Ben Holliday
Stear	Taken by James Sanders on Eagle Creek near Little Lick 22 jan 1825 Ben Holliday
10 Hogs	Taken by Thos. Hammons near Herndon's Mill 1 feb 1925 James Herndon
R & W Heifer	Taken by George Vallandingham on state road two miles from Owenton 28 feb 1825 Thos.L. Bryan

Bay   Taken by Samuel Coburn appraised $17.50 in specie
Filly   10 apr 1825 John Glass

Bay   Taken by John Quill near Campbell's Mill
horse colt 19 mar 1825   John Glass

Brown   Taken by Samuel Garvey on Wesly Creek a brown horse between
Horse   14 and 15 hands high 7 or 8 years old this spring a lump on his
               nose, a dimple or hole in his neck, one white spot on his left
               shoulder, spavined in his right leg, a scar above the hock of his
               left leg, scared by a string both hind buttock no brand
               appraised $0 4 jun 1825 Ben Holliday

Red   Taken by Thomas Cobb on Eagle Creek
Stear   nov 1825   William Cobb

Red   Taken by Wm. Jones on Eagle Creek
Heifer   1 nov 1825   Wm. Cobb

Gray   Taken by George Bath near Brinham's Mill on Cedar Creek
Horse   17 oct 1825 Peter Sanders

Red   Taken by James Redd on road from Jonas Jones to Robert
Heifer   Sanders 12 nov 1825 H.B.Gale

pg 65 (change in order of entry)

R & W   Taken by Selus B.Calvert on Cedar Creek near the Sulphur
Heifer   Lick 26 nov 1825

Brindle   Taken by Ellis Fitzgeral on Clark's Branch of Cedar
Steer   30 nov 1825

Red   Taken by Andrew Rogers on Cedar Creek
Heifer   3 dec 1825

Red   Taken by Charles Williams at Williamsburg
Heifer   6 dec 1825

Red   Taken by William Curry on Cedar Creek at the Sulphur Lick
Heifer   17 dec 1825 Peter Sanders

Bay   Taken by William Curry at the Sulphur Lick on Cedar Creek
Mare   17 dec 1825   Peter Sanders

two   Taken by Wm. Louderback on the Kentucky River opposite the
Ewes   mouth of 6 Mile Creek 20 dec 1825 Cassius Claxon

Red   Taken by Wm. Louderback on the Kentucky River opposite the
Stear   mouth of 6 Mile Creek 20 dec 1825   Cassius Claxon

Brindle   Taken by Thomas Carter at the mouth of Clay Lick Creek on the
Cow   Kentucky River 6 dec 1825   Cassius Claxon

Red   Taken by Wm. Thomas at the mouth of Clay Lick Creek on the
Heifer   Kentucky River 12 dec 1825 Cassius Claxon

R & W   Taken by Caleb Jones on road between Eagle Creek and Jonas
Heifer   Jones   Benj.Holliday

B & W   Taken by James Stewart on Brush Creek
Bull   Benj.Holliday

R & W   Taken by John Moore on state road two miles below New Liberty
Stear   17 dec 1825   H.B.Gale   JPOC

R & W   Taken by Michael Murry near Owenton
Stear   21 dec 1825   T.L.Bryan

R & W   Taken by William Hughes on Quill's Branch
Stear   apppraised $2.50 in specie   James Herndon

Red   Taken by William Linn near Herndon's Mill
Stear   16 nov 1825   James Herndon

Barrow   Taken by John Meek on the road from Owenton to the mouth
Hog   of Clay's Lick or Razor's Ferry about 4 mile from the former
              5 jan 1826   Cassius Claxon   JPOC

Ball face   Taken by William B. Forsee in the town of Owenton
Stear   16 jan 1826   B.Hayden

Brindle   Taken by George Jackson on Eagle Creek near the mouth of
Heifer   Two Mile appraised $4.50 in silver 7 jan 1826   H.B.Gale

R & W   Taken by Lewis Smithers on the Pond Branch
Heifer   7 jan 1826 Peter Sanders

Red   Taken by John Thomas on Kentucky River near the mouth
Heifer   of the Twins. 23 jan 1826 Cassius Claxon

Brindle   Taken by Edward George on Kentucky River opposite mouth of
Steer   Drennons Creek 24 jan 1826   Cassius Claxon

B & W   Taken by James Sale on the state road from Cincinnati to New
Heifer   Liberty three miiles from Eagle Creek 21 jan 1826

Red Heifer	Taken by Mary Moore on (Steels-Stut) road Ben Holliday
Black Steer	Taken by Samuel Cull near Kempers Mill on Twin Creek 21 jan 1825 Ben Holliday
Pided Stear	Taken by Jerry Perkins at the White Oak Lick on Elk Creek 4 feb 1826 James Herndon
Red Bull	Taken by Moses Altsman near Jones Lick 27 jan 1826 James Herndon
two Heifers	Taken by P.R. Jennings living near Thomas Woolfolks 4th feb 1826 H.B.Gale
Red Bull	Taken by George Marshall living on the Red Oak Fork of Eagle Creek 12 jan 1826 Benjamin Cave JPOC
White Stear	Taken by John Jennings on Eagle Creek 18 feb 1826 Ben Holliday
Three Hogs	Taken by William Blanton on Two Mile Creek three miles north of New` Liberty 27 mar 1826 Benj. Holliday
Grey Mare	Taken by Edward George living on the Kentucky River opposit mouth of Drennons Creek 2 jun 1826 Cassius Claxon
R & W Heifer	Taken by Daniel Lett on Three Forks 28 nov 1825 Wm. Cobb
Bay Horse	Taken by Benjamin Torn near Vallandingham's Mill Feb 1826 Moses Baker
2 Sows 12 pigs	Taken by Charles Johnson near Vallandingham's Mill 27 mar 1826 Moses Baker
White Heifer	Taken by Jesse Stamper near Cobb's Station 25 nov 1825 Wm. Cobb
Sorrell Horse	Taken by Thomas Hardin on Kentucky River about 3 miles above mouth of Cedar 15 may 1826 Peter Sanders
Bay Horse	Taken by Samuel O. Coburn on State road 2 miles from Heslersville 22 may 1826 B. Hayden
Bay Horse	Taken by James Vallandingham on road leading to Georgetown about one mile from Owenton 20 may 1826 B. Hayden

Black
Mare — Taken by Daniel Lett on (Thrace) Fork of Eagle Creek
6 may 1826   Wm. Cobb

Bay Stud
Colt — Taken by William B. Forsee in Owenton
30 jun 1826   B.Hayden

R & W
Heifer — Taken by Dennis Burns on Kentucky River about one mile
below mouth of Cedar Creek   27 nov 1826

R & W
Stear — Taken by Robert Jones on Kentucky River at the mouth of
(Poss) Branch   2 dec 1826

R & W
Cow — Taken by Celus Colvert on Cedar Creek near the Sulphur Lick
14 dec 1826

25 head
Hogs — Taken by Enis Harden on Kentucky River 2 miles above the
mouth of Cedar Creek   8 dec 1826   Peter Sanders

Roan
Mare — Taken by Lewis Smithers on (Poss) Branch brand CV
also stud colt   5 oct 1826   Peter Sanders

Black
Stear — Taken by William Jones near Payne's Bottom, also muley heifer
20 nov 1826   Wm. Cobb

Red
Stear — Taken by Joseph Rowlett on road from Owenton to Razors
Ferry on Kentucky River   11 dec 1826   Cassius Claxon

R & W
Stear — Taken by William Louderback in the River bottom half a mile
above William Ware's   16 dec 1826   Cassius Claxon

Red
Heifer — Taken by Albert Fears near Harrisburg about 3 1/2 miles from
from Owenton   20 nov 1826   Lydnor D. Hanks

Black
Horse — Taken by John Thomas on the Kentucky River near the mouth
of the Twins   30 sep 1826   Moses Baker

Two
Ewes — Taken by David Clyton at Cobb's Station
6 nov 1826   Wm. Cobb

Sorrell
Horse — Taken by Jesse Osburn on Eagle Creek
4 dec 1826   Wm. Cobb

B & W
? — Taken by Nathaniel Sanders-appraised by Geo.D. Sanders and
William Reed   9 dec 1826   H.B. Gale

Sorrell
Mare — Taken by Israel Ellis at Heslersville on the road leading from
Owenton to Georgetown 9 oct 1826   Cyrus Wingate

Red Bull	Taken by Peter Sanders near mouth of Cedar Creek 16 nov 1826 Cyrus Wingate
Wood Boat	Taken by John Marston on Kentucky River near mouth of Pond Branch- caught at the mouth of Cedar 6 jul 1826 Peter Sanders
pg 80 Red Stear	Taken by Andrew Carter near the mouth of Clay Lick 10 jan 1827 Cassius Claxon
Red Stear	Taken by Cassius Clanton near Kentucky River 7 miles west of Owenton 1/2 mile from mouth of Clay Lick 11 dec 1826 Lyndor D. Hanks
Sorrell Horse	Taken by George W. Sanders living at Sanders New Mill on Eagle Creek- appraised by Nathaniel Sanders and William Reed 18 dec 1826 H.B.Gale
Red Heifer	Taken by Richard (Sebre) one mile from Heslersville B. Haydon
9 Hogs	Taken by Absalom Joy on Big Twin Creek 1 1/2 miles above Vallandingham's Mill 10 jan 1827 Henry B. Gale
3 head Cattle	Taken by Richardson Osburn on Elk Creek 7 miles from Owenton appraised Jesse Stamper 28 nov 1826 Wm.Cobb
Red Stear	Taken by Joseph Roberts on New Castle Road 5 miles from Owenton 11 jan 1827 B.Haydon
Red Boar	Taken by Robert Snell one mile from Owenton 18 jan 1827 B. Haydon
Red Heifer	Taken by John McPherson one mile from Owenton 8 feb 1827 B. Haydon
Sorrell Mare	Taken by Alex Jackson on Main Eagle Creek 24 feb 1827 B. Haydon
Brindle Bull	Taken by Iverson Southword 24 mar 1827 Wm. Cobb
Ram Sheep	Taken by James Sanders on Eagle Creek near Sanders Upper Mill 10 feb 1827 Moses Baker
Red Stear	Taken by James Sanders same place 10 feb 1827 Moses Baker

B & W Boar	Taken by James Sanders same place 10 feb 1827 Moses Baker
Red Stear	Taken by William Howe 6 jan 1827 Wm. Cobb
B & W Barrow	Taken by Stephen Hughes 24 mar 1827 Wm. Cobb
Red Heifer	Taken by Keller Claxon on the ridge between Shortridge's Fork and Cedar Creek 29 jan 1827 Peter Sanders
Brindle Heifer	Taken by Enes Hardin on Kentucky River two miles above Cedar Creek 27 feb 1827 Peter Sanders
Horse & Mare	Taken by Charles Williams in Williamsburg 14 apr 1827
Bay Mare	Taken by Charles Williams in Williamsburg 30 apr 1827 Peter Sanders
Brindle Steer	Taken by James Stewart on Eagle Creek four miles from New Liberty 19 nov 1827 Moses Baker
Brindle Steer	Taken by William Ogden on Little Twin on road from Marion to New Liberty 17 nov 1827 Moses Baker
Red Cow	Taken by George Jackson on Eagle Creek 2 miles above Sanders Old Mill 24 dec 1827 H.B.Gale
Sorrell Colt	Taken by Belfield Glass on Caney Fork of Eagle Creek 24 jul 1827 R.G. True JPOC
3 head Hogs	Taken by John McPherson appraised by John Meek B.Haydon
Red Steer	Taken by Johnson ( ) (ink smear) near mouth of Cedar Creek appraised by Dennis (Byon) B. Haydon
Bay Mare	Taken by James Davis on Gains Branch of Eagle Creek 5 miles north of Jones Mill 5 miles from west of Million's Tavern on the dry ridge 4 dec 1827 Wilson B. Quill
White Weather	Taken by Benjamin Kemper at his mill on Twin Creek 26 dec 1827 B.Holliday
13 Sheep Cracked Bell	Taken by John Smith, post rider, Main Eagle Creek near Herndon's Mill 1 dec 1827 R.G. True

Red Cow   Taken by Jesse (Threlkeld-Shnelkeld-Hnelkeld) on Savern Creek
Calf   7 miles from Owenton 17 nov 1827 Cyrus Wingate

R & W   Taken by Thomas Balding on Brush Creek 19 jan 1827
Steer   B. Holladay

Red   Taken by Benjamin Runyon - torn by dogs-
Heifer   20 nov 1827 B. Haydon

Red   Taken by Israel Elligin at Heslersville
Bull   appraised by Samuel Cull. 5 nov 1827   B.Haydon

Heifer   Taken by David Maddon 4 miles north of Owenton on the Twin
Stear   2 dec 1827   Lydner D. Hanks

Spotted   Taken by Elijah Threlkeld 3 miles northwest of Owenton
Barrow   on the Twin Lydnor D. Hanks

Muly   Taken by John Bishop near New Liberty
Cow   17 dec 1827   H.B.Gale

Two   Taken by John McGibany
Cows   29 dec 1827 Wm. Cobb

Muley   Taken by Ray Sidebottom   27 oct 1827
Heifer   B. Haydon

R & W   Taken by Daniel Stewart on the New Liberty - Cincinnati road
Heifer   27 dec 1827 H.B.Gale

Hornless   Taken by George Wyant on Eagle Creek above Sanders Mill
Ram   15 dec 1827   H.B.Gale

Red   Taken by James Sanders 1 1/2 miles below Sanders Old Mill
Steer   1 mar 1828 H.B.Gale

One   Taken by James Sanders 1 1/2 miles below Sanders Old Mill
Ewe   1 mar 1828

one   Taken by Jonas Jones on his farm
Heifer   16 feb 1828   Ben Holladay

Cow   Taken by Robert (g true) near Joneses Mill on Main Eagle
Heifer   Creek   Wm. Cobb

Red   Taken by David Bibb in Thomases Bottom near the mouth
Steer   of the Twins 7 feb 1828   Cassius Claxon

Steer Cow	Taken by Cassius Claxon 9 miles from Owenton appraised Jas. Claxon 29 mar 1829 B. Haydon
Cow 2 Steer	Taken by Samuel Coburn 3 or 4 miles from Heslerville on Eagle Creek appraised by Samuel Cull 19 jan 1828 B. Haydon
Brown Mare	Taken by Nathaniel Sanders near Sanders New Mill appraised Samuel Smith 23 feb 1827 H.B. Gale
Bay Horse	Taken by John Hughs (senior) near Herndon's Mill on Main Eagle 2 apr 1828 Willson B. Gurl
Brown Mare	Taken by William Jones on Man Eagle Creek 22 apr 1828 Wm. Cobb
Bay Horse	Taken by John Wincott on the ridge between Shortridge Fork and Cedar Creek 18 may 1828 Peter Sanders
Sorrell Stud	Taken by Charles Clifton 6 miles east of Owenton 31 oct 1828 Wm. Cobb NOTICE: His gate is natural pace.
White Barrow	Taken by Richard Yancy between Owenton and New Liberty on state road 25 nov 1828 Lydnor D. Hanks
Red Steer	Taken by Noel Smithers 8 miles from Owenton 7 nov 1828 B. Hayden
Five Hogs	Taken by (Saml.) D. Vallandingham on state road two miles above Owenton 26 nov 1828 appraised $1.00 each by the subscribers: J.B.Vallandingham, S.P. Sims, B. Haydon
Sorrell Horse	Taken by Robert Southworth on Cany Fork of Eagle Creek 3 nov 1828 Robert G. True JPOC
Red Heifer	Taken by Tobias Wilhoite at Wilhoites Horse Mill 23 jan 1828 Peter Sanders
Muley Heifer	Taken by Alexander Guthrie near Wilhoites Horse Mill 8 jan 1828 Peter Sanders
Black Bull	Taken by Benjamin Matchter on Eagle Creek 3 nov 1828 Ben Holladay
Bay Mare	Taken by Franklin Osburn 28 mar 1828 Wm. Cobb
Red Heifer	Taken by Joseph George on the Kentucky River one mile above mouth of Jennings Creek 4 mar 1828 C.Claxon

Mare Filly	Taken by Uriah Chandler 4 miles east of Owenton 21 mar 1828 Wm. Cobb
Red Steer	Taken by Joseph Rowlet on the road leading from Owenton to Rasons Ferry 3 miles from latter 5 jan 1828 Cassius Claxon
Red Steer	Taken by George W. Davis near Herndon's Mill 29 nov 1828 Willson B. Guill
Old Cow	Taken by James Haydon on Mill Creek Old white pided cow, 16 dec 1828 Cassius Claxon
B & W Steer	Taken by William Lorance on Kentucky River in Thomas's bottom near mouth of the Twins 16 dec 1828 Cassius Claxon
Red Steer	Taken by Joshua Wilhoite on road from Owenton to Rasons Ferry 5 miles from latter 16 dec 1828 Cassius Claxon
Red Cow	Taken by Ray Sidebottom on road from Owenton to Georgetown 18 dec 1828 Robert G. True
Bay Filly	Taken by Charles Lett in Cobb's Station 1 jan 1829 Wm. Cobb
Brindle Stear	Taken by James B. Rogers on Steven's Creek 6 miles from Owenton on road to Williamtown appraised by James Maddox 29- - 1828 H.B.Gale
Bay Mare	Taken by George W. Sanders on road from Jonas Jones to Fredericksburg 3 jan 1829 H.B. Gale
Red Steer	Taken by David (Lines) appraised by Henry McDaniel and John McDaniel 15 dec 1828 John Brown JPOC
White Steer	Taken by Samuel Todd on road from New Liberty to Sanders Mill appraised by Wm. Fant 25 nov 1828 H.B.(Tate) JPOC
White Ewe	Taken by Andrew Ireland on Payne's Run 8 jan 1829 Wil. B. Guill
White Stear	Taken by Samuel Todd near New Liberty 25 dec 1828 John Brown
Black Bull	Taken by James H. Sale on road from New Liberty to Cincinnati 1 jan 1829 H.B. Gale
B & W Steer	Taken by John Vallandingham on state 1 1/2 mile north of Owenton 2 feb 1829 Sydnor D. Hanks

Brindle Bull	Taken by William Blanton 2 1/2 miles from New Liberty 31 jan 1829 H.B. Gale
Heifer	Taken by Richard H. Yancy on the road from Owenton to New Liberty appraised Philip Yancy 14 jan 1829 H.B. Gale
Two Steers	Taken by Belfield Glass on Cany Fork of Eagle Creek 14 jan 1829 Robert G. True
Bay Mare	Taken by Jacob Smith on Stevenes Creek 27 jun 1829 Thos. A. Benjamin
Red Heifer	Taken by John Gregory on the bridge in creek appraised by Absolum Ivy 17 jan 1829 H.B. Gale
Bay Mare	Taken by Charles Williams in Williamsburg 19 feb 1829 Peter Sanders
Gray Mare	Taken by Thomas A. Berryman 25 aug 1829 Sydnor D. Hanks
Red Heifer	Taken by Celus B. Calvert(Colvert) on Mathews Branch of Cedar Creek 2 dec 1829
Red Heifer	Taken by John Sander on Cedar Creek 27 dec 1828
	Taken by Tilson Tnissel(Snissel) of Indian Fork of Cedar 5 jan 1828
Red Bull	Taken by John Winscoat(Olinscoat) on ridge between Shortridge Fork and Cedar Creek 7 jan 1829 Peter Sanders
Red Heifer	Taken by Charles McFarland near Herndon's Mill 12 nov 1829 W.B. Guill
B & W Hog	Taken by Alvin Mothershead near Owentown 30 nov 1829 Thomas A. Berryman
4 head Cattle	Taken by Caleb Jones living near Edward Blanton 21 dec 1829 John Brown
Red Heifer	Taken by Charles Clifton E. Cobb JPOC
R & W Ster	Taken by Abraham Kelety E. Cobb

Muley   Taken by William Miller 2 dec 1829
Heifer   E. Cobb

Bay   Taken by John Jennings on state road at Eagle Creek
Horse   12 sep 1829 H.B. Gale

Red   Taken by P.R. Jennings near Sanders Old Mill
Heifer   1o nov 1829   Ben Holliday

Brindle   Taken by Jacob Ball near Jacob Hunter's Mill on the Big Twin
Heifer   30 dec 1829 John Brown

Gray   Taken by Benj. Haydon on state road between Owenton and
Filly   New Liberty 14 nov 1829 S.D.Hanks

Sorrell   Taken by William Stafford 3 miles below New Liberty on the
Horse   road to Sanders New Mill   25 nov 1829 H.B. Gale

Sorrell   Taken by Benjamin Massie near Herndon's Mill
Filly   5 jun 1829   Willson B. Guill

Bay   Taken by Samuel Todd near New Liberty on the road to Sanders
Mare   Old Mill 10 nov 1829 H.B. Gale

White   Taken by Elijah Martin 5 dec 1829
Hogs   E. Cobb JPOC

Red   Taken by Wm. Nowling near New Liberty
Heifer   1 jan 1829   John Brown

Gray   Taken by Lucy Spires on Kentucky River near mouth of Cedar
Mare   Creek 8 oct 1829 Peter Sanders

White   Taken by John McCoy near Kemper's Mill
Bearer   17 oct 1829   John Brown
(Barrow ?)

Bay   Taken by George B. Vallandingham from Owenton to
Mare   Georgetown 15 dec 1829   Thos. A. Berryman

Brown   Taken by John Montague on the road from New Liberty
Horse   29 jun 1829 H.B.Gale

Bay   Taken by William Lorance on Kentucky River near mouth of the
Mare   Twins in Thomas's Bottom   18 jun 1829 Cassius Claxon

Horse   Taken by John Glass on Main Eagle Creek
    21 nov 1829 Robert B. True JPOC

Stray Bull	Taken by Randal Jones on Eagle Creek above Sanders Old Mill 27 nov 1829 H.B. Gale
Bay Mare	Taken by Anthony Sparks at Sparkses Horse Mill 21 nov 1828 Peter Sanders
Brindle Bull	Taken by Cassius Claxton 10 miles west of Owenton near Kentucky River 4 dec 1829 Syndor D. Hanks
13 head Hogs	Taken by Asa Cobb on Eagle Creek 12 feb 1829 William Cobb
B &W Bull	Taken by Spencer Thomas near mouth of Clay Lick 20 jan 1820 C. Claxton
R & W Heifer	Taken by Richard H.Yancy on road from New Liberty to Owenton 30 jan 1820 Thos. A. Berryman
Red Steer	Taken by Harrison Monday 2 mile north of the bone lick 4 jan 1830 Syndor D. Hanks
R & W Heifer	Taken by John Green 5 miles below New Liberty to the left of road to Sanders New Mill 8 feb 1820 H.B. Gale
R & W Heifer	Taken by William Bowling 1/4 mile below New Liberty on the road to Madison 8 jul 1830 H.B.Gale
Old Cow	Taken by John Louderback the Clay Lick on the Kentucky River near Razons Ferry 20 jan 1830 H.B. Gale
Red Bull	Taken by William Barr on Kentucky River opposite mouth of 6 Mile Creek

END OF BOOK 1819-1830

Sanders,George W. 22,26
Sanders,James 16,17,22,
   23,24
Sanders,Nathaniel 21,22,25
Sanders,Peter,7,8,9,10,11,
   12,13,15,16,18,19,20,21,
   22,23,25,27,28,28,29
Sanders,Robert 6, 9, 17, 18
Sanders,Samuel 5
Scott,Robert 17
Scrimsher,John 1,2,3,4,5,6
Sebre,Richard 22
Selre,Richard 14

Shelton,Daniel 10
Shelton,David 13,16
Shelton,Hugh 8
Shipp,Colly 5
Sidebottom,Ray 15,24,26
Sims,S.P. 25
Smith,Jacob 27
Smith,John 1,7,8,23
Smith,Samuel 25
Smither,Robert 8
Smithers,Lewis 19,21
Smithers,Noel 25
Smott,William R. 3
Sneed,Polly 12
Snellll,John 13,16
Snell,Robert 22
Southwith,Robert 7
Southworth,Iverson 22
Southworth,Ivy 15
Southworth,Robert 25
Spanon,Richard L. 14
Sparks,Anthony 29
Sparks,Henry 6,9
Spicer,Cain 4,7,11
Spiers,Lucy 28
Spriers,Joshua 15
Squires,Caleb 9
Squires,John 9
Stafford,William 28

Stamper,Jesse 12,20,22
Stamper,Jonathan 9
Stephens,Benjamin 7
Stephens,Wilford 7
Stewart,Daniel 24
Stewart,james 8,19,23
Suiter,William 3,11,13
Swigert,John 11
Tate,H.T. 26
Thomas,John 19,21
Thomas,Spencer 29
Thomas,William 5,19
Thornton,George P. 12
Thornton,Perry 7
Threlkeld,Elijah 24
Threlkeld,Jesse 24
Tnissel,Tilson 27
Todd,Samuel 26,28
Torn,Benjamin 20
True,Robert G. 2,3,24,
   25,26,27
Tyler,Charles 2,4
Vallandingham,George 2,
   4,17
Vallandingham,George B. 28

Vallandingham,J.B. 25
Vallandingham,James 9,20
Vallandingham,John 3,26
Vallandingham,Samuel D. 25
Wamack,James 10
Ware,Walter 14
Ware,William 21
Warwick,James 1
Wilhite,Lewis 5
Wilhite,Tobias 7
Wilhoit,Lewis 4
Wilhoit(e),Tobias 4,26
Wilhoite,Joshua 26
Williams,Alexander 13,15
Williams,Charles 1,4,5,8,
   10,14,18,23,27
Williams,John 4

OWEN COUNTY, KENTUCKY STRAY BOOK 2 1830-1864

(a list of lost animals)

@ 1996
Carrie Eldridge
3118 CR 31 Big Branch
Chesapeake, OH 45619
fax: 614-867-3466

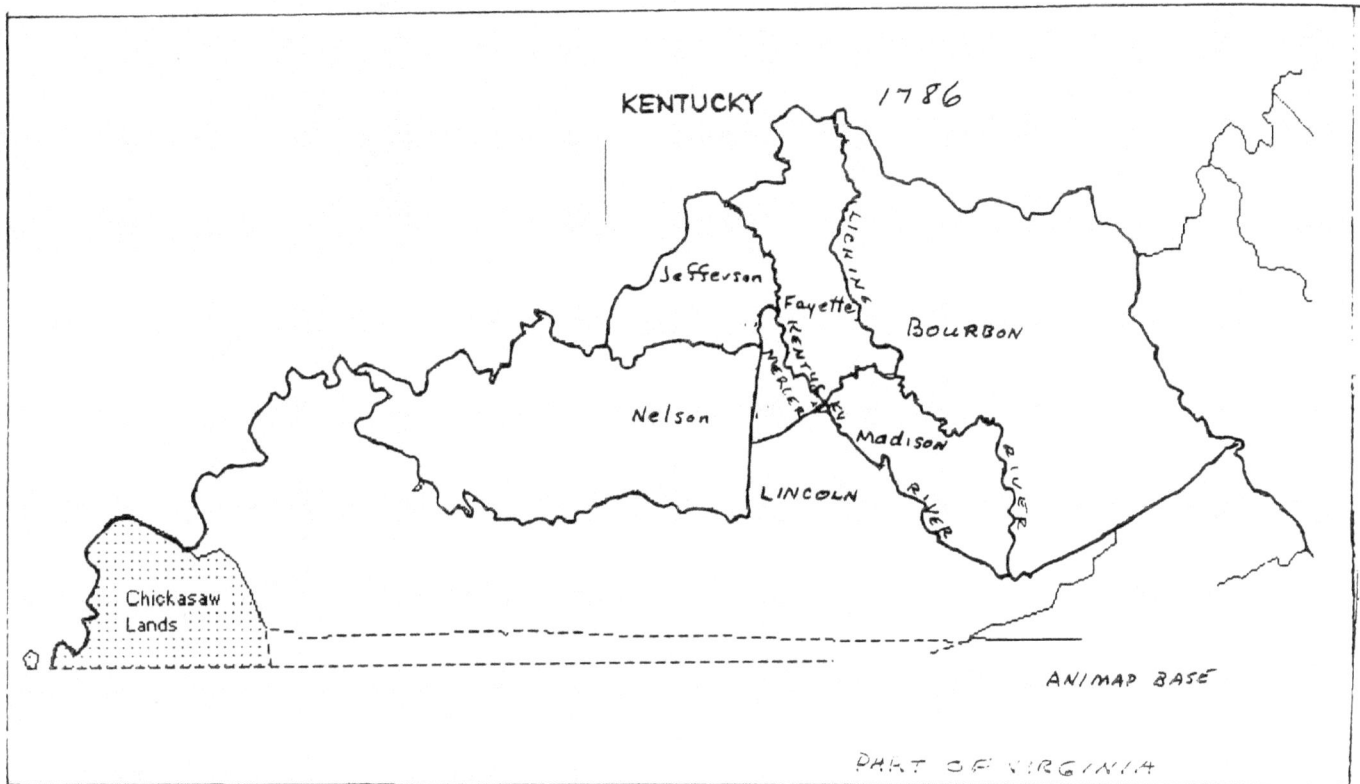

KENTUCKY 1786

Jefferson

Fayette

BOURBON

LICKING

Nelson

KENTUCKY RIVER

Madison

LINCOLN

RIVER

Chickasaw Lands

ANIMAP BASE

PART OF VIRGINIA

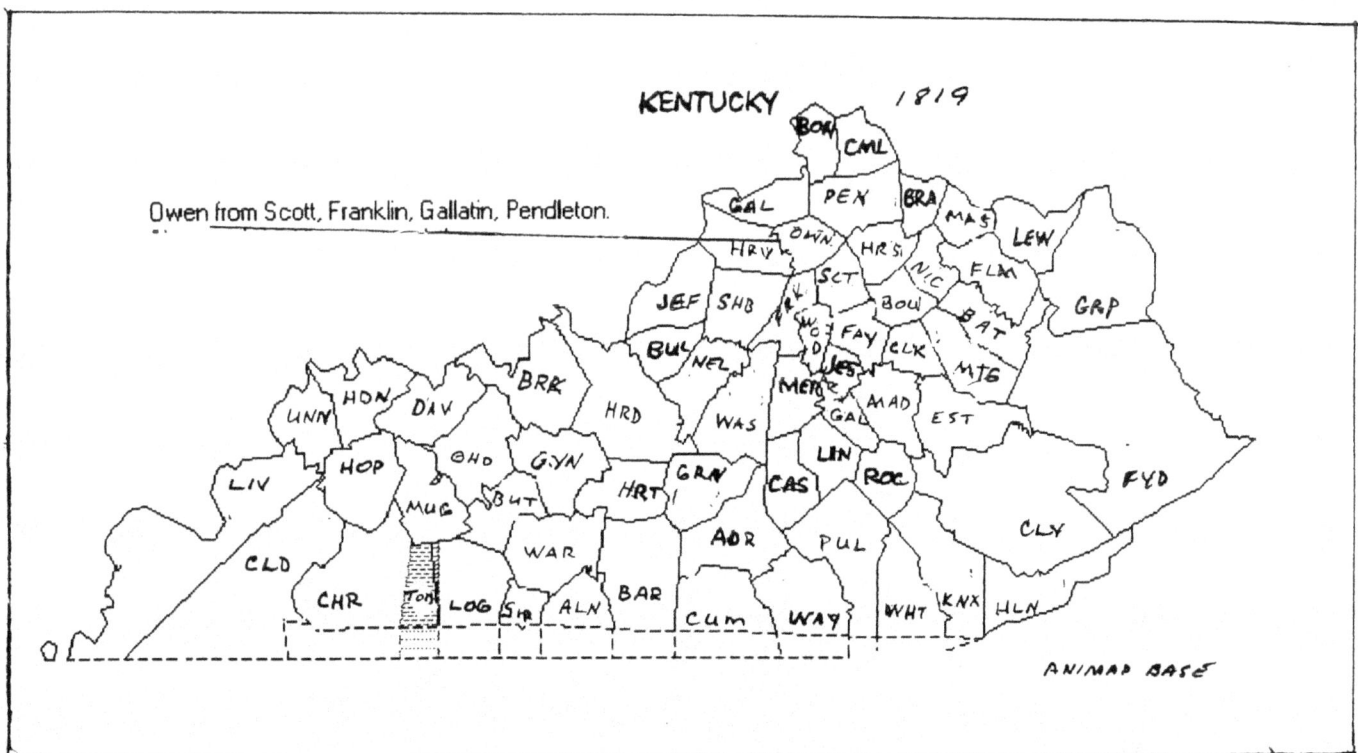

KENTUCKY 1819

Owen from Scott, Franklin, Gallatin, Pendleton.

BON
CML
GAL
PEN
BRA
MAS
LEW
OWN
HRV
HRSI
NIC
FLM
GRP
SCT
BOU
BAT
JEF
SHB
WOF FAY
CLK
MTG
BUL
NEL
JES
MER
GAL
MAD
EST
BRK
HRD
WAS
HON
DAV
LIN
ROC
UNN
GYN
CAS
FYD
OHO
HRT
GRN
LIV
HOP
BUT
ADR
PUL
CLY
MUG
WAR
CLD
TOR
BAR
CHR
LOG
SIM
ALN
CUM
WAY
WHT
KNX
HLN

ANIMAP BASE

Owen County, Kentucky Stray Book No.2

This gem is NOT a collection of odd or stray pages, but a listing of all the stray animals and an occasional boat that were claimed by individuals before the Owen County Justices.

Its importance lies in the locations given for the recovery of each animal, usually close to WHERE THE SETTLER LIVED.

This book identifies most of the physical features in Owen County and then locates a settler. This volume allows you to actually locate your ancestor not just verify he was in the county.

OWEN COUNTY, KENTUCKY

Located on the Kentucky River between Frankfort and Cincinnati, this county was a major byway in the nineteenth century . Today, it is isolated and the highway avoids the county seat, but Owen knows its history and any researcher will be delighted with its library and courthouse.

CABELL COUNTY, VA/WV

Bounded by the Ohio River, Cabell was the western most county in Virginia before West Virginia was created in 1863. The was also located on the James River Turnpike which connected Richmond with Lexington, KY.

Searching for personal family, I discovered a link between Owen County, KY and Cabell County, VA/WV. That connection is why this abstract of Stray Book 2 was made.

Surnames common to Owen County, Kentucky
and
Cabell County, (Virginia/West Virginia

In the late eighteenth century, John Pierce Duvall was a surveyor in Virginia who acquired much land in both Virginia and Kentucky. At his death he divided his vast holding among his various children who when to live on their land. One daughter Nancy received land in Cabell County, VA/WV, a son became the clerk of Owen County, Ky. Apparently, the son also had land in Cabell County and sold it to neighbors in Owen County.

Surnames found in Owen County, KY prior to 1840
which later appear in Cabell County, VA/WV

Adkins	Curry	Herndon	Runyon	Smith	Suter
Ayers	Duvall	Jordan	Sanders	Sparks	Syrus
Brown	Ellis	Perry	Sharp	Spears	Taylor
Brumfield	Garrett	Osburn	Shelton	Stevens	Vallandingham
Clark	Haydon	Roberts	Slaughter	Stribling	Wilson

Many of these names are common, but Ayers, Garrett, Haydon, Herndon, Sanders, Sharp, Stribling and Vallandingham all are found within a two mile radius of the old county seat Barboursville.

An obtituary for one of the Vallandinghams states he was born in Owen County, Kentucky.

Communities

Big Bone Lick in Boone Co.	New Columbus
Ghent	New Liberty
Harmony	*Owenton - county seat
Harrisburg	Popular Grove near Eagle Creek
Heslerville	Sparta
Marion on Kentucky River	Warsaw
Monterey	Williamsburg

Stamping Ground

Creeks, Streams & Rivers

Kentucky River
Ripple of KY River
Sand Ripple of KY

Owen County streams often flow into caves and are hard to follow

Cedar Creek of KY River	Eagle Creek
Ash Lick of Cedar	Caney Fork of Eagel
Cave Branch	Elm Lick Fork
Clarks Branch	Hamons Branch
Indian Fork	Lick Fork
Sulphur Lick	Mountain Island
	Paynes Run
	Ray Fork
	Red Oak Fork
	Three Forks of Eagle

other streams

Big Twinn	Brush Creek	Clay Lick near Ripple
Little Twin	Brushey Creek	Clay Lick Bottom
Twins near Mussel Shoal	Beech Branch	Caney Fork
Upper Twins	Big Seven Creek	Can Creek
	Black Cedar	Elk Creek

Long Lick Ford	Middle Fk of Indian	Richland Creek
Mashbe Creek	Possum Branch	Stevens Creek
Mosleys Creek	Poseum Ridge	Sturvs Creek
Meeks Bottom	Pond Branch	Slipery Creek Fork

Severn Creek   Three Forks
Two Mile Creek

STRAY BOOK 1830-1864   OWEN COUNTY, KENTUCKY

Sites, mills and meeting houses used for location

	page first mentioned
Aaron Ridge of Cedar Creek	8
Ameans or Emues Meeting House	3 & 7
Bibb's Farm	30
Branham's Mill on Cedar Ck near Claxon Ridge	4
Brock's Ford on Eagle Creek	5
Brown's Mill on Twinn Creek	33
Campbell's Mill	37
Castleman's Mill on Eagle Creek	7
Childer's Mill	22
Claxton Ridge	8
Clay Lick Ridge School House	28
Cobb's Mill on Eagle Creek	16
Cobb's Station on Richland Creek	25
Cobb's Station Road	37
Eagle Creek Ford	3
John Garvey's Ford	20
Green's Mill on Eagle Creek Warsaw Road	31
Greenup Fork Meeting House	22
Hamilton Bottom of KY River	26
Henlkills Mill (Shrelkill's)on Eagle Creek	4
Herndon's Mill	3
Hunter's Mill on Big Twinn	3
Jones' Mill on Main Eagle Creek	13
Jones' Upper Mill on Main Eagle Creek	5
R. Kemper's Mill on headwaters of Twin	22
Jos. R. Lee's Mill on Main Eagle Creek	20
Lock No.3 on KY River	23
Lusby's Mill on Beech Branch	32
Macedonia Church	34
Malloy's Mill	38
Meek's Ferry on KY River	22
Old Steam Mill on Brush Creek	37
Pleasant Ridge Meeting House	25
Popular Grove Meeting House	25
Pore House Farm	39
Razor's Ferry near Clay Lick Flat	2
Roses(Ross's) Mill on Eagel Creek	32
Runnoldses Mill on Eagle Creek	40
Sanders Lower Mill on Eagle Creek	13

Sanders New Mill on Eagle Creek	7
Sanders Old Mill on Eagle Creek	2
Sanders Upper Mill on Marion Road	5
Smith's Mill on Eagle Creek	38
Spark"s Bottom of KY River	26
Stamper's Mill	33
Walker's Factory	31
Weatherses Mill	2
Wilhoite's Horse Mill between Cedar & Severn Creeks	6
Woodfork's Bottom of KY River	28

book begins on page 110
> Each entry describes the animal exactly, but to conserve space
> only location and biographical information is retained. (see p42)
> Location is usually where the person is living.
> Last name is Justice of Peace for Owen County.

Bay Horse	Taken by Isaac Webster on Clarks Branch of Cedar Creek 29 jun 1830 Peter Sanders
Cow & Calf	Taken by Sherwood Maddox north of Owenton near road to Big Bone in Boone County. 19 nov 1830 S.D.Hanks
Brindle Cow	Taken by Johnson Ballard on Kentucky River near mouth of Cedar Creek 7 nov 1829 Peter Sanders
R & W Steer	Taken by William Smithers on Pos-- Branch 6 feb 1830 Peter Sanders

p111

Bay Mare	Taken by Caleb Jones on Mosbys Creek 17 apr 1830 Benjamin Holaday
Chestnut Sorrel	Taken by William Barns near Rick Vallandingham's on Big Twin Creek 21 apr 1830 John Brown JBOC
Muley heifer	Taken by William Richardson on Ray Fork of Eagle Creek 27 feb 1830 Robert G. True
R & W Steer	Taken by John Moore on road from New Liberty to Sanders Old Mill on Eagle Creek 24 feb 1830 Ben Holaday

p112

Sorrel Horse	Taken by Henry Rogers on Cedar Creek one mile from the Sulphur Lick 29 oct 1830 Peter Sanders
Black Mair	Taken by W.S.Ballard on Kentucky River near Sand Ripple 20 may 1830 Peter Sanders
Blew Sow	Taken by Henry (Simon) Carter in Clay Lick Flat near Rasors Ferry 13 feb 1830 C. Claxon *Henry Simon Carter*
Sorrel Filly	Taken by Diana Conn 7 miles NE of Owenton on the road to Weatherses Mill (18 oct 1830)??

p113

R & W Bull	Taken by Richardson A. Osburn on Elk Creek 9 nov 1830 Thomas A. Berryman
Heifer	Taken by John Smith near Cobb's Station 15 dec 1830 E.Cobb
Red Steer	Taken by Harrison Monday 2 1/2 mile north of Owenton on Cincinnati Road 28 dec 1830 S.D.Hanks
Black Bull	Taken by John Holbrook 5 dec 1830 E.Cobb

p114

12 head Hogs	Taken by William Cobb 12 dec 1830 E. Cobb
Red Steer	Taken by Uriah Chandler 5 dec 1830 E. Cobb
Black Cow	Taken by Walter Adkins 4 miles from Jonas Jones 29 nov 1830 Jas.H. Sale
R & W Steer	Taken by Lewis Ayers on road from Jonas Jones to ford on Eagle Creek 18 dec 1830 Jas. H. Sale

p115

Black Cow	Taken by William Taylor on Kentucky River near Marion 18 dec 1830 S. Calvert
Pided Steer	Taken by John Gregory on Big Twin 4 miles south of New Liberty 18 dec 1830 S. Calvert
R & W Heifer	Taken by John Bishop 2 miles north of New Liberty on waters on Two Mile Creek 25 dec 1830

p116

Spotted Hog	Taken by Samuel Todd one mile NW of New Liberty 23 dec 1830 S. Calvert
Sow & Pigs	Taken by Joseph (Shilman) 1 feb 1831 S.D. Hanks

Bay
Mare
Taken by Harrison Munday 2 1/2 miles north of Owenton on Cincinnati road 3 jan 1831 S.D.Hanks

Sorrel
Mare
Taken by James Simpson near Marion on Kentucky River 14 jun 1831   John Brown

p117
Bull
Taken by William Long on Big Twin near Hunter's Mill Road 3 dec 1830 John Brown

Stray
Taken by John (Absted) near Hunter's Mill on Big Twinn has Small bell with Morris Mathers on it 30 dec 1830 John Brown

Sorrel
Horse
Taken by James Sanders on Eagle Creek below Sanders Old Mill 20yrs old 8 jan 1831 Ben Holliday

p118
Sorrel
Horse
Taken by James Wood near Emues(?) Meeting House 24 jan 1831 John Brown

Spotted
Hog
Taken by Joseph Rowlett on road from Owenton to Razon's Ferry 3 miles from Razon's apprasied by John Meek & Delvin Walker 19 feb 1831 C. Claxton

White
Bull
Taken by Robert Thomas on Kentucky River near mouth of The Twin --

p119
Red
Bull
Taken by John Murray 4 1/2 miles south of Owenton on main Severn Ck 8 jul 1831 Lydnor D. Hanks

Brown
Filly
Taken by Colby Holbrook near Herndon's Mill 25 apr 1831 H.B. Quill

Bay
Horse
Taken by Daniel Stewart 1 mile from the ford on Eagle Creek on road to Cincinnati appraised by James Brock & James Carlton 9 May 1831 Jas. H. Gale

p120
Black
Filly
Taken by Ezekiel Ritchey on Severn Creek 4 jun 1831 Jacob H. Smith

Sorrell Horse	Taken by William Bramlett on Ash Lick Fork of Cedar Creek 26 day 1831 Peter Sanders
Sorrell Colt	Taken by James Wilson on Lick Fork of Eagle Creek 17 nov 1831 Robert G. True
4 head Hogs	Taken by John G. Williams 2 miles from Branhams Mill on road to Frankfort 2 nov 1831 Peter Sanders

p121

Red Heifer	Taken by William Howe on Eagle Creek 28 nov 1831 N.M. Bacon
Brown Cow	Taken by Thomas B. Dillon in Owenton appraised by Benj. Runyon & Paschal Todd 5 nov 1831 N.M. Bacon
9 head sheep	Taken by Simeon Jackson on Eagle Creek near Henlkills Mills 26 nov 1831 Robert G. True
B & W Hog	Taken by Angus Alexander on Three Forks 5 dec 1831 Elisha Cobb
W & B Hog	Taken by Uriah Chandler 22 nov 1831 Elisha Cobb

p122

12 head sheep	Taken by John Glass near Long Lick Fork 4 dec 1831 Robert G. True
one Sheep	Taken by John C. Bacon - appraised by Wm. McSute & R.M. Duvall 12 dec 1831 N.M. Bacon
Sorrell Mare	Taken by John Spears in Owenton appraised by J.C. Bacon & Alvan (Mothe) 9 dec 1831 N.M. Bacon
Red heifer	Taken by Azariah Roberts 9 mile south of Owenton near state road to Frankfort within 1/4 mile of Tobias Wilhoites home 10 dec 1831 Sydnor D. Hanks

p123

Bull Calf	Taken by Wm. Long near Hunters Mill on Big Twin Creek appraised by Absolum Ivy 3 dec 1831 John Brown

Bay Mare	Taken by John W. Works near Jones Upper Mill on Main Eagle Creek 12 dec 1831 W.B. Guill
Red Bull	Taken by Jeremiah Garvey on road from Jonas Jones to Fredericksburg 29 dec 1831 Jas. H. Sale
White Sow	Taken by Dicy Devon 10 dec 1831 C. Claxton

p124

Sows Shoats	Taken by Jesse Stamper 25 dec Elisha Cobb
Brindle Heifer	Taken by James Sanders on road from Marion to Sanders Upper Mill 12 dec 1831 James H. Sale
W & B Sow	Taken by Wauler Garrett 5 dec 1831 Elisha Cobb
Spotted Barrow	Taken by Reuben Crouch on Eagle Creek near Broch's Ford appraised by William Jackson 10 nov 1831 John Brown

p125

Heifer Calf	Taken by Absolum Ivy near Hunters Mill on Twin Creek appraised by Wm. Long. 3 dec 1831 John Brown

I have today settled with Joel Herndon, paymaster fo the 100th Reg. Ky Militia & find him indebted to said Regiment in the sum of $4.51. Given under my hand 29 jan 1831 Jas. H. Sale Col.100th Reg. KY Militia   (1832 ?)

Brindle Steer	Taken by Cassius Claxton 9 miles west of Owneton and below Razon's ferry 2 jan 1832 S.D. Hanks
Two Hogs	Taken by Bryan O'Banion near (Shrelkill) Mill on Eagle Creek 22 dec 1831 Robt. G. True

p126

Brindle Yearling	Taken by Thomas Lutes (Sutes-Leetes) 10 dec 1831 J.H. Smith
Gray mare	Taken by William Haddon 1/2 mile from Owenton at the forks of Lexington/Frankford road 22 sep 1832 N.M. Bacon

Red Heifer Taken by Jacob Hesler near Owenton
3 jan 1832

p127
R & W Cow Taken by John Redding on Indian Fork of Cedar
30 nov 1831 P. Sanders

Red Bull Taken by Jeremiah Spires in Wiliamsburg
13 jan 1832 P. Sanders

R & W Steer Taken by John Robinson on Middle Fork of Indian Creek
18 jan 1832   P. Sanders

Black Steer Taken by Uriah Chandler
15 jan 1832   N.M. Bacon

Bay Horse Taken by Jacob H. Smith on Owenton/Cincinnati Road two miles
from Owenton 10 jan 1832 S. D. Hanks

p128
7 head Hogs Taken by William Rowlett at mouth of Savern Creek
appraised by Joseph Geott & Robert Smithers
9 jan 1832 C. Wingate

4 head Hogs Taken by John Parker at the crossing of Eagle Creek to
Castleman's Mill 18 feb 1832 J.H. Sale

Bay horse Taken by Joseph M. Thomas on wateers of Brush Creek on the
Williams Town road 21 apr 1832 J.H. Sale

p129
Black Mare Taken by Tobias Wilhoite at Wilhoites Horse Mill between
Cedar & Severn Creeks 2 may 1832 P. Sanders

3 Hogs Taken by John Vallandingham near Owenton
18 may 1832 N.M. Bacon

Gray Mare Taken by James Wilson on the Owenton/Lexington road 2 miles
above Heslersville 18 may 1832 R.G. True

Rone Mare Taken by Brumfield Long on Caver Branch of Cedar Creek
5 jul 1832 P. Sanders

p130

Muley
Bull
Taken by Jonas Jones on the New Liberty/Cincinnati road
5 mar 1832   J.H. Sale

2
Horses
Taken by John Stonestreet 6 miles from Owenton near Clay's
Lick 24 spe 1832 N.M. Bacon

gray
Horse
Taken by William Haddon 1/2 mile from Owenton at fork of
Frankfort/Lexington road 22 sep 1832 N.M. Bacon

Red
Heifer
Taken by Williams Perkins
21 nov 1832 E. Cobb

p131

five
Hogs
Taken by Obadiah Wilhoite 2 miles from Owenton on the
Frankfort road 27 nov 1832 N.M.Bacon

R & W
Heifer
Taken by John Absher on Big Sevin Creek
16 nov 1832 John Brown

Bay
Horse
Taken by John T. Baker near Sanders New Mill on Eagle Creek
15 dec 1832 John Brown

p132

Brown
Mare
Taken by Daniel Shelton within two miles of Ameans Meeting
House on Big Seven Creek 1 dec 1832 John Brown

Black
Steer
Taken by William Barr at Clay Lick Flat of KY River
22 dec 1832 N.M. Bacon

11 head
Hogs
Taken by William Barr living at the Clay Lick Flat on KY River
opposite the mouth of 6 Mile 22 dec 1832 C.Claxon

Grey
Horse
Taken by James Herndon at the Mountain Island on Eagle
Creek 1 may 1833 R.G.True

Brown
Mare
Taken by John Parker at the crossing of Eagle Creek leading
to Castlemain's Mill 9 jan 1833 J. Sale

Brindle
Heifer
Taken by Joel Herndon on the road from Owenton to New
Liberty 5 jan 1833 M.N. Bacon

Spotted
Hog
Taken by Joseph Perry at the Popular Grove
25 feb 1833 J.H. Sale

p134

R & W   Taken by Calistine Claxton on Claxton's ridge
Steer   18 feb 1833 Peter Sanders

R & W   Taken by George B. Vallandingham 2 mile from Owenton
Heifer   on the Georgetown/Owenton road 23 feb 1833 N.M. Bacon

Red   Taken by Ellis Fitzgerald on Clarkes Branch of Cedar Creek
Heifer   28 mar 1833 Peter Sanders

Bay   Taken by Richard Williams appraised by (Jonas) Duvall
Filly   and Oliver (Sonles) 25 feb 1833 J.H. Sale

p135

Gray   Taken by James Herndon at the Mountain Island
Horse   1 may 1833 Robt. G. True

Bay   Taken by Moses Dixon at the Clay lick Flat near the ripple
Mare   14 may 1833   C. Claxton

Sorrell Taken by Daniel Smith 2 miles from New Liberty
Horse   JPOC

p136

Bay   Taken by John (Acbhes?)
Horse   20 jul 1833 E. Cobb

W & R   Taken by Benj. Runyon
Bull   appraised Joseph F. Hawkins - 20 jul 1833 J.H. Smith

Steer   Taken by Tobias Wilhoite on Frankfort/Owenton road and
Bull   9 miles from Owenton 2 nov 1833 S.D. Hanks

B & W   Taken by George Razor on the Owenton road 3 miles from
Heifer   Razor's ferry appraised by David Crable and Jas.W.Rowlett
         23 nov 1833 C. Claxon

p137

Red   Taken by Levin Eatherton on Savern Creek
Heifer   29 nov 1833   Cyrus Wingate

R & W   Taken by Mrs.Robinson on head waters of Cedar Creek
Bull   appraised by Absolum Clark & Adam Hiter 7 dec 1833
         G. C. Brinham

Steer Calf	Taken by Thomas Bromley near New Liberty 12 dec 1833 John Brown
11 Sheep	Taken by Mullison Sparks on the KY River 27 dec 1833 G. C. Brinham
p138 Brindle Cow	Taken by Geo.B. Vallandingham 2 miles from Owenton on the Lexington road 28 dec 1833 N.M. Bacon
Red Cow	Taken by William M. (Satin) near Owenton 8 jan 1834 N.M. Bacon *William M. Satin*
White Sow	Taken by Charles Williams at the mouth of Cedar Creek appraised by John Spires and William (Tolen) 11 jan 1834
p139 Blue Barow	Taken by Lucy Spires on Kentucky River 14 jan 1834 G.C. Brinham
Bull 2 Steers	Taken by Alexander (Rey--) on Kentucky River at Marion 26 feb 1834 John Brown *Alexander Rigg* *Rigg*
Sorrel Mare	Taken by John Spires near mouth of Cedar Creek appraised Peter Sanders & Henry Clark 6 may 1834 G.C. Branham
p140 Sorrel Horse	Taken by George Marshall on Caney Fork 8 mar 1834 E. Cobb
Spotted Hog	Taken by John Holbrook 24 mar 1834
Sorrel Mare	Taken by Thomas Carter on the Twins near the Mussel Shoals on Kentucky River 10 mar 1834 C. Claxton
Brown Mare	Taken by Thomas Carter on the Kentucky River near the Mussel Shoal apprasied by Harvey Clark and James Claxton 10 jun 1834 C. Claxon
p141 Bay Mare	Taken by Reuben Smith on Aaron Ridge of Cedar Creek- 3 miles from KY River appraised by Samuel Sanders and Robert Smith 10 jun 1834 C. Claxton

Brown
Horse   Taken by Tobias Wilhoite 9 mile s from Owenton on the
             Frankfort road 20 may 1834 Sydnor D. Hanks

Sorrel
Horse   Taken by John Ballard on Kentucky River
             12 aug 1834   G.C. Branham

p142
Sorrel   Taken by John Spires near mouth of Cedar Creek appraised by
Mare   Peter Sander & Henry Clark 6 may 1834 G. C. Branham

Bay   Taken by Ray Sidebottom on the Georgetown/Owenton road
Horse   appraised by Tobias Wilhoite & John Leonard
             12 aug 1834 Cyrus Wingate

Two   Taken by John Sparks near mouth of Cane Creek on KY River
Fillies appraised by Maddison Sparks and Denis Syrus
             29 sep 1834 G.C. Branham

p143
Gray   Taken by Ellis Fitzjarrel on Cedar creek appraised by
Mare   James (Robeas) Bromfield (Song) 15 sep 1834

Sorrel   Taken by Thomas Carter on Kentucky River near Mussel Shoals
Mare   appraised by John Meek and Aaron Green 27 oct 1834 C.Claxon

Bay   Taken by John Vallandingham one mile from Owenton
Filly   on New Liberty Road 3 nov 1834 N. M. Bacon

Brindle Taken by Jacob Hesler near Owenton
Steer   19 nov 1834 N.M. Bacon

p144
One   Taken by Jon C. Bacon in Owenton, appraised by Jos.F. Hawkins
Heifer   and H.D. Bohannon 24 dec 1834   N.M. Bacon

2 Sorrel Taken by Charles Sonthoite 3 1/2m from Owenton on the
Horses   Frankfort Rd 24 dec 1834 N.M. Bacon

Bay   Taken by Henry Clarke 6m from Owenton on Frankfort Rd
Mare   22 dec 1834 N.M. Bacon

p145
B & W   Taken by Ellis Fitzarel on Black Cedar Ck 5m from mouth
Heifer   26 dec 1834   J.C. Branham

Black Hog	Taken by Willis Bates on Cedar Creek 8 dec 1834 J.C. Branham
Brindle Bull	Taken by Thomas Carter on Upper Twins near the Muscle Shoal apprasied by Jordan Thomas and Douglas Rigg 13 dec 1834 C. Claxon
Red Steer	Taken by John Vallandingham 1 1/2m from Owenton on the Cincinnati Rd apprasied by Joel Herndon 19 dec 1834 J.H. Smith

(hand writing is deplorable)

p146

Brindle Cow	Taken by Thomas Suter on Stevens Crak 1m from home appraised by F. Smith 7 jan 1835 J.H. Smith
Three Hogs	Taken by William (Haddon) on Lexington Road 10 jan 1835 N.M. Bacon *William Bacon*
R & W Heifer	Taken by Charles J. Wilhoite 3m from Owenton on the Frankfort road 1 jan 1835 N.M. Bacon

p147

R & W Heifer	Taken by Henry Elliot near Herndon's Mill 4 jan 1835 W.B. Quill
Sorrel Mare	Taken by Robert Sanders near the mouth of Clay Lick appraised by William Ervin and John Meek 26 jan 1835 C. Claxon
Red Steer	Taken by Robert Sanders on Kentucky River near the mouth of Clay Lick appraised by John Meek and Moses (Down) 8 dec 1834 C Claxon *Moses Down*

p148

White Steer	Taken by William Garrett 6m from Owenton on the Warsaw road 30 nov 1834 S. Calvert
Pied Heifer	Taken by R. H. Yancy on the Owenton/New Liberty Road 14 dec 1834 S. Calvert

p149

R & W Heifer	Taken by John Jennings at the Eagle Creek crossing on the New Liberty road 11 jan 1834 S. Calvert

Red Bull	Taken by James C. McDaniel on Kentucky River near Marion 29 nov 1834 S. Calvert
Sorrel Mare	Taken by Samuel Todd on road from New Liberty to Sanders Old Mill 1 dec 1834 S. Calvert
White Steer	Taken by Charles Kemper on the Owenton/New Liberty Road 20 dec 1834 S. Calvert
White Bull	Taken by David (Maaaa-Madda) near (Hawsburg) _Harrisburg_ on the road from Owenton to Warsaw 30 jan 1835 J.Calvert

David Maaaa

p150 Bay Horse	Taken by Samuel Todd road from New Liberty to Sanders Old Mill 10 jan 1835 S. Calvert

****

I Joseph Caldwell certify that I solemized the rites of matrimony between (Mens) Brumfield and (Dannda) Sharp 25 apr 1833 Baptist Church
********** _Mens Brumfield   Dannaa Sharp_

Roan Mare	Taken by William Barr at Clay Lick Bottom 1 jun 1835 N.M. Bacon
Brown Mare	Taken by John Speirs near mouth of Cedar Creek 20 may 1835 S.C. Branham
p151 Red Bull	Taken by Thomas Hancock 2m from Owenton 7 feb 1835 N.M. Bacon
W & R Heifer	Taken by George B. Vallandingham 2m from Owneton on the Lexington road 5 mar 1835 N.M. Bacon
Sorrel Mare	Taken by (Keer) Jackson near Sanders New Mill on Eagle Creek appraised by Thomas (---------) and John Street 8 aug 1835 John Brown

H B Huoald

p152 Sorrel Horse	Taken by John H. Dews at Heslerville appraised by H.B.(Huoald) and William (Brown) 25 mar 1835 N.M. Bacon

William Hern

Red Steer	Taken by (James) A. Hearn on Steven Creek 6m from Owenton apprasied by Jacob (Irossion) 16 feb 1835 J.H. Smith

James A Hearn   Smit Jarp Sun

R & W   Taken by Jessy (Dellander) near Hunters Mill on Twin Creek
Steer   22 nov 1834 John Brown

p153
B & W   Taken by (J----) Wilson at the fork near Jones Mill
Steer   27 feb 1835 W. B. Smith

Horse   Taken by Hezekiah Jackson near Sanders Lower Mill on Eagle
Colt   Creek 6m from New Liberty 25 aug 1835 S. Calvert

Bay   Taken by Jas. E. McDaniel near Marion
Horse   23 may 1835 S. Calvert

use original

P154

W & B	Taken by John (Abston) near Hunters Mill on Twin Creek
Steer	appraised by Wm. King 18 dec 1835 John Brown

B & W	Taken by David Shelton on (green) of Sevrin Creek
Heifer	2 dec 1835 Cyrus Wingate

White	Taken by Samuel Mason 1/2m from Owenton
Steer	7 dec 1835 N.M. Bacon

B & W	Taken by Robt. Clark (a man of color)
Hog	2 nov 1835 N.M. Bacon

p155

R & W	Taken by John H. (Deus) at Heslersville
Heifer	30 nov 1835 N.M. Bacon

R & W	Taken by Thomas Hardin on KY River 3m above mouth of
Steer	Cedar Creek 20 nov 1835 G.C. Branham

R cow &	Taken by Azariah Roberts on Claxton's ridge 3m from G.C.
Calf	Branham's Mill 21 nov 1835 G.C. Branham

p156

Bay	Taken by John Ingram
Horse	27 nov 1835 E. Cobb

Red	Taken by Bartlett B. Mason near Herndons Mill
Heifer	26 dec 1835 E. Cobb

Red	Taken by Hiram Stamper
Heifer	28 dec 1835 E. Cobb

Sorrel	Taken by John (Bowen/Brown) 5m from Owneton on Frankfort
Mare	road appraised Wm. Brown/Bowen and Ellis Wilson
	7 dec 1835 N.M. Bacon

p157

Steer	Taken by Garland Sims
Heifer	7 dec 1835 J.H. Smith

Black	Taken by Obadiah E. Wilhoite appraised by John B. Hancock
Heifer	7dec 1835 J.H. Smith

Bay Mare
& Colt
Taken by Russell Robison on Cedar Creek
16 nov 1835 G.C. Branham

p158
Sow &
Pigs
Taken by Luke (ton) 3m Owenton
4 jan 1836   N.M. Bacon

Red
Bull
Taken by Levi Griffin 1m from Owenton on New Liberty Rd
4 jan 1836   N.M. Bacon

R & W
Bull
Taken by George B. Vallandingham 2m from Owenton
on Lexington Rd   9 jan 1836 N.M. Bacon

Spayed
Sorel
Taken by John T. Fulson on the Owenton to New Liberty Rd
18 jan 1836 N.M. Bacon

p159
R & W
Steer
Taken by Thomas Hardin on KY River 3m from mouth
of Cedar Creek 20 nov 1835 G.C. Branham

Black
Steer
Taken by John Redden on Cedar Creek 7m above
Branham's Mill 9 jan 1836 G.C. Branham

Red
Heifer
Taken by John B. Calvert on Cedar Creek 5m above
Branham's Mill 5 dec 1835 G.C. Branham

Black
Sow
Taken by William Hughs Sr. near Jones Mill on Main Eagle
Creek 16 jan 1836   Wilson B. Guill

p160
Red
Heifer
Taken by John Lowderback near Caly Lick Flat on KY river
14 dec 1835   W.H. Smith

Bay
Mare
Taken by Thomas Gregory near Hunter's Mill on Levin Creek
8 jan 1836 John Brown

p161
R & W
Cow
Taken by Nancy Smith on Main Eagle Creek near Mountain
Island   4 feb 1836 W.B. Guill

Grey
Horse
Taken by William Thomas near mouth of Savern Ck, apprasied
A.J. Sparks & Wm. Munston 27 feb 1836 N.M. Bacon

Brown   Taken by Leonard J. Fleming on Claxon's Ridge 4m from G.C.
Mare   Branham's Mill 16 apr 1836

p162
Sorrel   Taken by John H. (Devi) at Heslersville
Mare   25 apr 1836 N.M. Bacon

Bay   Taken by Daniel Bibb on Kentucky River
Mare   30 apr 1836 Jas. Smith

Sorrel   Taken by Benj. Haydon 10m from Owenton on Lexington Road
Colt   14 amy 1836   N.M. Bacon

Mare &   taken by Thomas Jones near Cobb's Mill on Eagle Creek
Colt   20 may 1836 N.M. Bacon

p163
Gray   Taken by Ray Sidebottom on road from Owenton to the
Horse   Stamping Ground half way   23 may 1836 G.C. Branham

Black   Taken by Obadiah Sheets on Serveren Creek on the Owenton to
Horse   Frankfort Road   20 oct 1836 C. Wingate

Bay   Taken by Jno. C. Bacon - apprasied by Jno. McFerson Sr. &
Mare   John Brown   1 dec 1 836   J.D. McClure

p164
White   Taken by James F. Theobald 2 1/2m west of Owenton
Hog   4 dec 1836   Jas. Smith

Black   Taken by James Ford between Owenton & New Liberty
Heifer   appraised by Wm. Hatton and Ben Ford 24 dec 1836
         J.D. McClure

White   Taken by William Smith on Pnd Branch 2m from Branham's
Hog   Mill 28 dec 1826   G.C. Branham

p165
Bay   Taken by Richard Williams near Cedar Creek
Colt   28 dec 1836   G. C. Branham

R & W   Taken by David Hoover 6m above Branham's mill
Steer   14 apr 1837   G.C. Branham

Sorrel Horses	Taken by William Curry Sr. 4m above the mouth of Saw Creek 7 aug 1837 G. C. Branahm
Black Mare	Taken by Duncan Ellis near warehouse of John -- on KY River (many calius) appraised by Solomon Jones and L. McAndrew 20 oct 1837 John Brown
p166 Bay Mare	Taken by Polly Wilhoite on Savern Creek 7m from Owenton on Frankfort Road appraised by N.M. Bacon and Smith Wingate 28 oct 1837 J.D. McClure
Brindle Steer	Taken by Nimrod B. Sebree on Richland Creek 10m from Owenton appraised by William Lynn and Charles Clifton 24 nov 1837 Cyrus Wingate
Two Heifers	Taken by Benj. Haydon 10m from Owenton to the road to Stamping Ground 15 dec 1837 Lewis White
p167 Red Heifer	Taken by Whit Ballard on Kentucky River 16 dec 1837 G.C. Branham
Speckled Heifer	Taken by Benj. Stephens near mouth of Cedar Creek 16 dec 1837 G.C. Branham
4 Head Sheep	Taken by Robt. Smithers on Pond Branch one mile from KY River 7 dec 1837 G. C. Branham
R & W Steer	Taken by (Mat) Burns on Frankford road 13m from Owenton 29 dec 1837 G.C. Branham
p168 White Heifer	Taken by Luke Covington on Cedar Creek 15m from Owneton 5 feb 1837 Lewis White
Hogs Barrow	Taken by William (Gnyon) on Cedar Creek 5m east of G C. Branham's Mill 14 feb 1837 G.C. Branham
Two Steers	Taken by Francis A. Duvall 1 1/2m from Jos. R. Lee's Mill on Main Eagle Creek appraised by Jos. Lee & Chas. Duvall 3 mar 1838 Lewis White (3 mar 1837 at bottom)

p169

R & W Yearling	Taken by Nancy Wilson 9m from Owenton 15 mar 1838 Lewis White
Bay Mare	Taken by Benj. Haydon 10m from Owenton on Stamping Ground Road -14m from Stamping Ground appraised by H.B. Glass and Absolum Clarke 13 jun 1837 Lewis White
Black Mare	Taken by Maj. Ben Haydon on state road from Owenton to Georgetown 29 sep 1838 J.C. Scott
Brindle Steer	Taken by Henry Clarke on Severn Creek 31 dec 1838 Cyrus Wingate

p170

Seven Hogs	Taken by Saml. J. Baker appraised by Thos. Johnson 27 dec 1839 John Brown
White Hog	Taken by Thos. Cumble on road from Warsaw to Owenton 8 dec 1838 J. Garvy
R & W Heifer	Taken by John McKensey on Brushy Creek on the New Liberty/ Williamstown road 14 dec 1838 Jas. Smith
Pided Heifer	Taken by Alfred Molone appraised by Wm. J. Harrison 12 dec 1838 J.H. Smith

p171

Black Steer	Taken by Elijah Stewart on Stevns Creek on Owenton/ Williamstown road appraised by Andrew Harrison 7 dec 1838 J.H. Smith
Bay Mare	Taken by Samuel S. Bond 4m from New Liberty on the road to Cincinnati 4 jan 1839 S. Calvert
Hog	Taken by (Pelly) (Lovejoy) 22 dec 1838 S. Calvert

p172

Brindle Heifer	Taken by William Crawford 4m from New Liberty on the road from Warsaw to Big Bone Lick 22 dec 1838 S. Calvert

Hog

Taken by Walter Garnett 4m from Owenton on the Warsaw road
13 dec 1838 S. Calvert

Red
Heifer

Taken by Thos. McKensy 3m east of New Liberty
1 dec 1838 S. Calvert

Brindle
Bull

Taken by Jas. Brock near the Jump Off on the road from New
Liberty to Cincinnati   9th - 1838   S. Calvert

Red
Bull

Taken by T. Searcy 1 1/2m from New Liberty on the Cincinnati
road   28 nov 1838   S. Calvert

p173
5 head
hogs

Taken by B. J. Kemper on the New Liberty to Owenton road
24 nov 1838   S. Calvert

Chesnut
Horse

Taken by John Whitaker on KY River 3m below Marion
17 nov 1838 S. Calvert

R & W
Heifer

Taken by John Whitaker on KY River 3m below Marion
19 nov 1838   S. Calvert

13 head
Sheep

Taken by Samuel Todd near New Liberty
3 nov 1838   S. Calvert

p174
R & W
Steer

Taken by John B. Hudson on Cedar Creek 3 1/2m above
Branham's Mill 13 dec 1838   G. C. Branham

R & W
Heifer

Taken by Bexfield Glass on a fork of Eagle Creek
20 dec 1838   Lewis White

Gray
Mare

Taken by Jas. (O'Neal) near Owenton appraised by Isaac
Brown and James (Hearn) 13 jul 1838 J.D. McClure

p175
Bay
Horse

Taken by B. Haydon on the road from Owenton to the
Stamping Ground   28 jul 1838 J.C. Scott

Red
Steer

Taken by Sandford Johnson near New Liberty
14 feb 1839   L. Garvy

Rone
Mare

Taken by George Perry on (Masbe's) Creek
5 feb 1839   J. Garvy

Two Sheep	Taken by John L. Garvy living near John Garvy's ford 22 (jan) 1839

p176

Sorrel Horse	Taken by Matthew Latta appraised by Wm. Glass & George White 23 nov 1838 J.C. Scott
Red Steer	Taken by Peter Wigington on road from Owenton to Warsaw 16 jan 1839 J.C. Smith
Red Steer	Taken by Thomas A. Berryman 25 mar 1839 J.D. McClure
Red Cow	Taken by James (Willton) on Cedar Creek appraised by Wm. Brown - G.C. Branham

p177

White Heifer	Taken by Ellis (Litz Land) on road from Frankfort to little mouth of Cedar 22 mar 1839 G.C. Branham
White Steer	Taken by Tobias Willhoite on road from G.C. Branham's mill to Owenton 9 feb 1839 G.C. Branham
Gray Mare	Taken by Thomas (Brmble) near Jonas Jones 10 may 1839 J. Garvy

p178

Justice of the peace appeared and appointed
Richard H. Shipp 12 oct 1839 J.H. Smith

Cyrus Wingate, Justice certifies Joel Herndon and Alvan
Mothershead commissioners to settle accounts of administrators
1 oct 1839 C. Wingate

White Heifer	Taken by Belfield Glass on Cany Fork of Eagle Creek 15 nov 1839 Lewis White
Bay Horse	Taken by Wm. Louderback on Clay Lick 14 jul 1839 W. H. Smithers

p179

Sorrel Mare	Taken by John Quisenberry near Meek's Ferry 2 jul 1839 W.H. Smither

R & W Steer   Taken by Granville Garrett on Cincinnati road east of New Liberty appraised by Jas. E. Kenny & John O. Jones 17 dec 1839 (J.B. English)

Brindle Heifer   Taken by Belfield Glass on Cany Fork of Eagle Creek 28 nov 1839 Lewis White

p180
R & W Heifer   Taken by Henry Calvert on the New Liberty to Ghent road appraised by S. Alte & G. W. (Allsmith) 17 dec 1839 J.B English

Sorrel Horse   Taken by Samuel Todd on the New Liberty to Ghent road appraised by John McNeal & James H. Calvert 17 dec 1839 J.B. English

Dunn Filly   Taken by Jacob H. Holiman about 4m from New Liberty on the Marion road appraised by William Lumer & Joseph Thomas 9th (mar) 1839 J. B. English

no 181
p182
B & W Heifer   Taken by John Riddle on the Williamtown road appraised by S. Hall 15 nov 1839 J.B. English

Red Steer   Taken by Samuel Todd on the road from New Liberty to Sanders Mill apprasied by R.H. Todd 1 dec 1839 L. White

W & R Yearling   Taken by Geo. Marshall on right fork of Eagle Creek 21 dec 1839 L. White

B & W Heifer   Taken by Granville Robinson on Indian Fork of Cedar 31 dec 1839

p183
Bay Mare   Taken by Gideon Wood appraised by B. Glass & T. (ASerwall) 21st day 1840 J.C Scott

Red Steer   Simon Tufts on Indian Fork 20 dec 1839 Lewis White

Muly Heifer   Taken by Uriah Chandler on Sturus Creek 11 Jan 1840 J. H. Smith

Red   Taken by John McKinsie 7m from New Liberty
Cow   14 feb 1840   James Smith

p184
Red   Taken by Virgil West on the road from Greenup Fork Meeting
Bull   House to Heslersville   9 mar 1840   Cyrus Wingate

White   Taken by Jno. F. Williams 6m from Owenton
Barrow   18 feb 1840   James Smith

Bay   Taken by Isreal Wilhoite on head waters of Severn Creek
Mare   appraised John Wilson & John B. Hancock 5 aug 1840
           J.H. Smith

Two   Taken by Jesse Barker on Cedar Creek
Heifers   4 nov 1840   Lewis White

p185
Bay   Taken by (Chaus) Claxon 1 1/2m east of Meeks Ferry and KY
Mare   River   apprasied John Thomas & William Thomas
           28 apr 1841   James Smith - Thos. A. Ritchey

Red   Taken by Jemason Garret on headwaters of the Twin 1m from
Heifer   B. Kemper's Mill appraised Jas. Willson 8 Jan 1841
           Thos.A. Ritchey

p186
2 white   Taken by Thos. Brown near New Liberty appraised by A. Bradney
Sows   9 may 1841   Thos. A. Ritchey

Black   Taken by James Pryor 5m from Owenton on the road to
Steer   Childer's Mill   9 jan 1841   James Smith

Red   Taken by W.M. Maddox near Popular Grove
Heifer   25 jan 1841   J. Garvy

p187
R & W   Taken by Samuel (Stiger) near Jonas Jones
Heifer   25 jan 1841 J. Garvey

R & W   Taken by Frances Moore near Robert Bonds
Cow   25 jan 1841 J. Garvey

W & R Heifer	Taken by John F. Williams on Brushy Creek 6m north of Owenton appraised R.F. Squires 2 mar 1841 Jas. Smith

p188

Bay Mare	Taken by William Linn on Ritchland Creek 2m from Herndon's Mill appraised by Jacob Hesler & James Maxwell 10 apr 1841 John D. McClure
Sorrel Horse	Taken by Alexander Moore on head waters of Twin Creek 2 1/2m from Owenton appraised by Hearlison Munday and William Teal 15 apr 1841 J.H. Smith
Sorrel Horse	Taken by Benjamin Martin near Cobb Mill on Main Eagle Creek 4 jun 1841 Asa Cobb

p189

Roan Horse	Taken by Lewis Morgan on the three forks of Eagle Creek 11 sep 1841 Asa Cobb
Red Heifer	Taken by Benjamin Hayden on State Road 11m from Owenton 27 nov 1841 Lewis White
Red Steer	Taken by George B. (Linerson) on Elm Lick Fork of Cedar 20 nov 1841 Lewis White *George B. Linerson*

p190

R & W Steer	Taken by Benjamin Stevens opposite Lock #3 on the KY River appraised Alexander Williams 29 nov 1841 G.C. Branham
Black Steer	Taken by James Davidson 4m from mouth of Cedar Creek on the Frankfort/Owenton road 6 nov 1841 G.C. Branham
Pided Heifer	Taken by William (LDvngan) on Cedar Creek 5m from mouth 5 dec 1841 G.C. Branham

p191

Brindle Steer	Taken by Thomas Brown near New Liberty, appraised by C.W. Davis and Lewis Veal 9 dec 1841 Thos. H. Ritchey
Red Heifer	Taken by Ambrose C. Hancock on Stevens Creek 18 dec 1841 J.H. Smith
Red Steer	Taken by Robt. Burk on Big Twinn 1m from Hunter's Mill appraised by B.D. Johnson 24 dec 1841 Thos. H. Ritchy

p192

Red
Bull   Taken by Samuel Todd on Ghent Road 1 1/2m from New Liberty
appraised by Samuel Roher 6 jan 1842   Thos. H. Ritchey

Brindle
Steer   Taken by James E. McDaniel 1m below Marion on KY River
24 jan 1842   John J. Baker

Red
Steer   Taken by Henry Webster on Cedar Creek 7m from mouth
appraised by Jacob Webster   5 feb 1842 G.C. Branham

p193

R & W
Heifer   Taken by L.J. Fleming on Cedar Creek 4m from mouth
appraised by Reuben Smith 24 dec 1841 G.C. Branham

R & W
Steer   Taken by T.H. Ream 7m from Owenton on the Williamstown
road 28 jan 1842 Jas. Smith

R & W
Steer   Taken by Absalem Hardin on Cedar Creek 3m from mouth
appraised by C.P. Sanders   17 dec 1841 G.C. Branham

p194

2 Bullls
Steer   Taken by Murphy on KY River 1m below Marion
15 feb 1842 Jno. J. Baker

Bay
Horse   Taken by Thomas Gregory on south fork of Big Twin
appraised by S.D. Evans and James Wilson 25 may 1842
Thomas H. Ritchey

p195

Roan
Mare   Taken by Thomas Carter on Poseum Ridge
21 may 1842   H. Giles

Sorrel
Mare   Taken by James Claxon in Meeks Bottom on KY River
28 jun 1842 H. Giles

Bay
Mare   Taken by Jessee Suter 3m NE of Owenton
10 aug 1842   J.H. Smith

Two
Fillies   Taken by Hulden Lewis on Stamping Ground road 4m from
mouth of Cedar 17 sep 1842   G. C. Branham

p196

Gray
Horse   Taken by W.R. Abbott on Mane Eagle Creek 1m from Mountain
Island   19 sep 1842   Lewis White

Sorrel Horse	Taken by Benjamin J. Smith 2m NE of Pleasant Ridge Meeting House on Stephens Creek 29 sep 1842 James Smith
Bay Horse	Taken by Lydid Chandler 5m NE of Owenton 5 oct 1842 A.sa Cobb
Sorrel Horse	Taken by Mathew Latts on Cany Fork of Eagle Creek 15 oct 1842 Lewis White

p197

Three Steers	Taken by John Williams on Eagle Creek 3m from Cobbs Mill 9 nov 1842 Asa Cobb
Red Steer	Taken by E. W. Smith on Elk Creek near Cobbs Station 12 nov 1842 Asa Cobb
Steer Yearling	Taken by Sanderson Mason on Eagle Creek 3m above Cobbs Mill 12 nov 1842 Asa Cobb
R & W Steer	Taken by William Lynn on Richland Creek near Cobbs Station 19 nov 1842 Asa Cobb

p198

B & W Heifer	Taken by Joshua Stamper 3m below Cobbs Mill Asa Cobb
Red Heifer	Taken by James Herndon at Herndons Mill 3 dec 1842 Asa Cobb
Black Steer	Taken by James Sharpe on Cany Fork of Eagle Creek 2 dec 1842 Lewis White
Brindle Steer	Taken by George B. Jemmerson on head waters of Cedar Creek 17 dec 1842 Ben Haydon
Spotted Yearling	Taken by Joseph Caldwell on Brush Creek 1 1/2m from Popular Grove Meeting House on the New Liberty to Williamstown road 17 dec 1842 J.B. English

p199

Brindle Steer	Taken by L.T. Fleming on Cedar Creek 4m from mouth appraised by C. Claxon and R. Smith 29 dec 1842 G.C. Branham

Red Heifer	Taken by Lewis Ayrs 7 jan 1843 J. Garvy
Brindle Steer	Taken by Willis Oliver on Indian Fork of Cedar Creek 4m above mouth appraised by C. P. Sanders 9 jan 1843 G. C. Branham

p200

Black Mare	Taken by Isaac Webster 4m from mouth on Cedar on the Frankfort/Owenton road appraised by S. B. Calvert & John S. Smith 12 jan 1843 G. C. Branham
Mare Colt	Taken by Rial Thomas near Popular Grove Meeting house 13 jan 1843 J. Garvy
Brindle Steer	Taken by Henry Welch on Opossum Ridge 26 jan 1843 H. Giles

p201

Roan Steer	Taken by Thos. Carter on Opossum Ridge 27 jan 1843 H. Giles
2 Red Heifers	Taken by Edmund Walden at Hamilton Bottom on KY River 28 feb 1843 H. Giles
R & W Steer	Taken by John (Bendles) on Greenups Fork Creek 6 mar 1843 John (Bonm)
Bay Mare	Taken by Rob. Smither on Pond Branch 7 apr 1843 G. C .Branham

p202

Brown Horse	Taken by Wm. E. Neal on Red Oak Fork of Eagle Creek 4 may 1843 Lewis White
Brown Horse	Taken by John H. Suter about 3 1/2m SE of Owenton 8 aug 1843 Jas. Smith

p203

To the County Court of Owen County: Please remove the names of Wm. Montgomery, Elijah C. Curry, Edmd. Poe, Harlin H. Ford and Morgan B. Clinn as trustees of the United Baptist Church of Jesus Christ at the mouth of Cedar Creek by the request of the Church 4 Saturday in February 1844 J.B. Cathrit clk, James E. Duvall min (??)

R & W   Taken by Peter Hale on Paynes Run of Eagles Creek
Steer   8 dec 1843   J.C. Glass

Red   Taken by Henry (Webster) 1m south of Heslersville
Heifer   25 dec 1843 B. Haydon   *Henry Webster*

W & R   Taken by Uriah Kateman 3m from mouth of Cedar Creek
Cow   16 dec 1 843   G.C. Branham

p204
W & R   Taken by Wm. (Loules) 3m from Branhams Mill adjoining *Coates?*
Steer   Tobias Wilhoites 16 dec 1843 G.C.Branham *W Loules*

W & R   Taken by Jacob K. Smith 3m NE of Owenton appraised by C.
Steer   (Bainlnap) 18 dec 1843   Joel Herndon
      C Bainlnap

Pided   Taken by Benj. J. Smith on Stevens Creek 6 miles E of Owenton
Steer   appraised by J.C. Ginn 2 nov 1843

p205
Brindle Taken by B. J. Smith on Stevern Creek 6 miles East of Owenton
Bull   20 nov 1843   Jas. Smith

Brown   Taken by Andrew Hearn on Stevern Creek
Filly   14 oct 1843   Jas. Smith

One   Taken by (Jn) Clark on head waters of Cedar Creek
Sheep   7 nov 1843   B. Haydon

W & R   Taken by W. (TAbram) 2 miles west of Herndon's Mill
Heifer   16 nov 1843   Asa Cobb

p206
R & W   Taken by John W. Clark on Elk Creek
Steer   18 dec 1843 B. Haydon

R & W   Taken by Gabriel (Thnkald) on Severn Creek
Heifer   6 jan 1844   John (Bowen/Brown) *Wm Bown*

Pided   Taken by Robt. Jones 7 miles east of New Liberty on the Owenton
Steer   to Williamstown road apprasied by R.T. Squires and
       W. Catterson 20 mar 1844 F. Brown *F. Brown*

B & W   Taken by Wm. Brown on Severn Creek
Steer   23 mar 1844   John (Bowen)

p207
Muley   Taken by Patsy Smoot in Sparks Bottom on KY River
Cow   2 jan 1844   H. Giles

Red   Taken by Willis Bates at Clay Lick Flat
Heifer   2 jan 1844   H. Giles

Red   Taken by Thomas Carter on Clay Lick Ridge near the school
Heifer   house 26 dec 1844 H. Giles

White   Taken by Robert Thomas
Boar   26 dec 1844 H. Giles

p208
Bay   Taken by Wm. M. Suter in Owenton apprasied by Lindsey
Horse   Briscol and Phillip Thornton 15 jun 1844 Joel Herndon

W & R   Taken by Lewis Simpson on headwater of Richland Creek
Steer   8 mile from Owenton 25 oct 1844 B. Haydon

Muley   Taken by Hugh Slutton on the Owenton to New Liberty road
Cow   15 jan 1845   Joel Herndon

p209
R & W   Taken by Jeremiah Perkin on Elk Creek 7 mile east of
Steer   Owenton 22 nov 1844 Asa Cobb

Brindle   Taken by John Watkins 3 miles below mill on Eagle Creek
Steer   14 dec 1844   Asa Cobb

R & W   Taken by F. Simons on 3 forks of Eagle Creek 8 miles east
Steer   of Cobbs Mill 14 dec 1844 Asa Cobb

2 Red   Taken by Spencer Carter in Woodforks Bottom on KY River
Steers   10 jan 1845   H. Giles

Sorrel   Taken by (Kimbro) Sanders
Mare   10 jan 1845   H. Giles

p210
Red
Cow   Taken by Sanford Johnson 2 miles west of New Liberty
              appraised by Willis Coates & Edwind Miner
              1 jan 1845   F. Brown

Piped   Taken by Miller Garrettt 3 miles east of New Liberty
Steer   20 jan 1845   F. Brown

Sorrel   Taken by Charles Clifton on Richland Creek 8 miles south of
Mare   Owenton 3 apr 1845   Asa Cobb

Gray   Taken by John (Brindle) on (Severn) Creek 12 miles from
Mare   Owenton 27 may 1845 B.Haydon

p211
Sorrel   Taken by Abraham Simpson 9 miles from Owenton on the
Mare   Georgetown road   20 may 1845 B. Haydon

Gray   Taken by Smith Taylor on Hamons Branch of Eagle Creek
Mare   7 jun 1845   B. Haydon

p212
White   Taken by James Simmons 14 miles from Owenton on Cedar
Steer   Creek   28 nov 1845   B. Haydon

Brindle   Taken by Wm. Brown on Slipery Creek Fork 3 miles from
Steer   Owenton 4 dec 1845   B. Haydon

Red   Taken by James Adkins near Popular Grove Meeting House on
Heifer   the Cincinnati road 13 dec 1845 R. L. Edwards

p213
Sorrel   Taken by B.J. Kimper 1 `/2 mile south of New Liberty
Horse   10 jun 1846   F. Brown

Sorrel   Taken by Jno. Holbert on Sheels road 4 miles from Owenton
Horse   18 may 1846 B. Haydon

Bay   Taken by Robert A. Jameson on head waters of Cedar Creek
Horse   16 miles from Owenton 5 jun 1846 B. Haydon

p214
Red   Taken by Jno. R. (McFenny) 5 miles from Owenton near
Steer   Williamstown road oct 1845 Jno.D. McClure (5 aug 1846)

Bay
Horse
Taken by B. Haydon on the Owenton to Georgetown road
appraised Solomon Whitcomb and M.D. Briscoe
8 nov 1845 Jno. D. McClure

Sorrel
Filly
Taken by R. W. Rowland 8 miles east of Owenton on Eagle
Creek 11 nov 1845

p215
Sorrel
Mare
Taken by Jacob Musselman on 3 Forks of Eagle Creek
13 feb 1846   J.C. Glass

Red
Heifer
Taken by Ray Sidebottom on Steels road 5 miles from Owenton
appraised John B. Hancock 4 dec 1846   Joel Herndon

Cow
Taken by David Grable on Little Twin Creek 2 1/2 miles from
mouth, one milch cow, 4 dec 1846 H. Giles

p216
Bay
Filly
Taken by Jeremiah Garvey near Popular Grove
20 nov 1846 R.L. Edwards

Bay
Mare
Taken by Mason Burk on road from New Liberty to Sanders
New Mill appraised by R.R. Revill and J.M. Ferguson
8 may 1847 Thos. H. Ritchey

Brindle
Steer
Taken by William Hawkins on Severn Creek appraised by
Rowland Kendall and George Exter   15 nov 1847

p217
Black
Steer
Taken by James Ellis near Grenups Folk meeting house
11 dec 1847 B. Haydon

Red
Heifer
Taken by Barret Noel near Popular Grove
227 nov 1847 R.L. Edwards

Bay
Mare
Taken by John Thomas on Eagle Creek near Popular Grove
27 dec 1847   R.L. Edwards

p218
R & W
Cow
Taken by Thomas M. Sales on the road from New Liberty
to Garrett's Mill appraised by Lytte McHatton and
William Garrett 18 dec 1847 Wm. McHatton

Black Steer	Taken by James Wood in Meeks Bottom 15 jan 1848 H. Giles
Brindle Heifer	Taken by J.M. Walter at Walters formerly Bibbs ferm 15 jan 1848 H. Giles
White Heifer	Taken by John L. Castleman near the NE corner of the county 10 feb 1848 R.L. Edwards
p219 Bay Mare	Taken by James Wright on road from William L. Trobridge's to Walker's factory 18 feb 1848 John (Bowne)
Spotted Steer	Taken by Wm. Lusby near Harrisburg appraised by P.H. Todd & E. Bainbridge 21 feb 1848 Joel Herndon
Bay Mare	Taken by Samuel S. Bond appraised by Thomas Brown & James P. Orr 11 sep 1848 Jno. B. (Musevy)
p220 Red Steer	Taken by J.S. Wilhoite on the Owenton/Frankfort road appraised by Charles S. Wilhoite & R.C. Noel 20 nov 1848 Wm. McHatten
Dunn Bull	Taken by David Claxon in Meeks Bottom 23 nov 1848 H. Giles
Red Heifer	Taken by James Carlten near NE corner of county 24 jan 1849 R.L. Edwards
p221 Roan Steer	Taken by A.V. Edwards near NE corner of county on Eagle Creek 24 jan 1849 R.L. Edwards
Bay Horse	Taken by Charles Hesman on the road from Owenton to Greens Mill on Eagle Creek 2 miles from mill appraised by Thomas True and Wm.J. Hughs 14 may 1849 Joel Herndon
Red Heifer	Taken by H.B. Gale near New Liberty appraised by R.H. Gale and R.R. Revill 16 jun 1849 F. Brown
p22 Stone Boat	Taken by as a stray on the KY River at the primises of Lausin Schooler 60' long & 16' wide appears to be coal boat 1 feb 1850 H. Giles 9 feb 1850

Red   Taken by A. Mothershead 1/2 mile East of Owenton appraised
Steer   by Wm. Roberts & David Conder   27 nov 1852 Wm. McHatton

Red   Taken by R. Sidebottom 5 miles from Owenton on the Stamping
Cow   Ground road 4 dec 1852 Wm. McHatton

p223
Red   Taken by Wm. (Bowsn) 5 miles S of Owenton on the Frankfort
Steer   road 29 dec 1852 Wm. McHatton

Yearling   Taken by Wm. L. Trobridge
Bull   29 dec 1852 Wm. McHatton

Brindle   Taken by Anderson Wilhoite on Severn Creek 1 mile above
Steer   Rankin's Mill   18 dec 1852 Wm. H. Hill

p224
2 yr old   Taken by James Simpson 4 miles from Lusbys Mill near the
Steer   Grant line appraised George Simpson
            24 dec 1852 W.C. Warring

2 yr old   Taken by Lewis Ayers near Popular Grove
Steer   18 nov 1852   Jno. S. Snape

Bay   Taken by John Brock near Popular Grove
Mare   17 dec 1852   Jno. S. Snape

p225
Fat   Taken by Richard Steward living near Dr. John Stackhouse
Hog   2 miles from Popular Grove appraises by Richard Steward Jr.
            20 dec 1852   Jno. S. Snape

Sorrel   Taken by Wm. Lewis near Green's Mill on the Warsaw Road
Mare   2 1/2 miles from Roses Mill on Eagle Creek
            28 dec 1852 J.S. Snape

Pale   Taken by C.H. Duvall on the road from Lusbys Mill to New
Bull   Liberty appraised by W. C. Ransdell 4 oct 1852 W.C.Warring

p226
Red   Taken by Doctor R. Kinnon on the road from Lusbys Mill to
Heifer   Georgetown appraised by Sanderson Mason
            20 oct 1852 W. C. Warring

Sorrel Mare	Taken by Hugh Stamper near Stampers Mill 7 jul 1852 H.S. Stamper
Red Cow	Taken by Jess McFerron 1 1/2 mile north of Owenton on road to Lusbys Mill appraised by Wm. McPherron & John Lusby 30 aug 1852 Wm. McHatton

p227

B & W Hog	Taken by John McFerron Sr. (found 1 jan 1852) 1 1/2 mile NE of Owenton on road to Lusbys Mill appraised by Wm. McFerron 26 aug 1852 Wm. McHatton
Pided Heifer	Taken by Jacob Razor in Meeks Bottom on KY River appraised by J.E. Coo(per) and Joseph Razer 12 dec 1852 S.F. Williams
Brown Horse	Taken by Waller Garrett 3 miles E of New Liberty appraised by J.M. Coats & J. White 228 oct 1850 F. Brown

p228

Red Heifer	Taken by Thomas Hardin on KY River 3 miles above Monterey appraised by George Bates Sr. & Jesse Scrimsher 14 nov 1851 S. Sanders
Roan Horse	Taken by T.G. Haskins near Greenups Meeting House 10 nov 1851 Saml. Sanders
Bay Horse	Taken by Thomas May 3 miles west on New Liberty on Twin Creek (6 yr old) 1 dec 1852 J.M. Coates
Bay Horse	Taken by Thomas May 3 miles west of New Liberty near Twin Creek (12 yr old) 1 dec 1852 J.M. Coates

p229

Bay Horse	Taken by Reuben L. Thomas on road to Owenton 2 1/2 miles from Browns Mill 29 jun 1853 J.M. Coates
Sorrel Mare	Taken by Tobias Wilhoite on Severn Creek 3 miles from Monterey 13 apr 1853 S. Sanders
Sorrel Mare	Taken by Jesse L. Green 20 aug 1853 Jno. S. Snape

p230

Brindle Steer Taken by Joseph Baker near Ross' Mill on Eagle Creek appraised by S. R. Ayers 2 dec 1853   Jno. S. Snape

Red Heifer Taken by Moses Altzman appraised by Wil Holbrooks Nov.1st 27 dec 1853 G.W. Hammons

Bay Horse Taken by A.P. Wever 2 dec 1853 G.W. Hammons

p231

Black Heifer Taken by Thos. A. Berryman near owenton 24 nov 1856 J.L. Hill

White Steer Taken by J.M. Clark appraised by J.A. Wilhoite & M. Hall 21 jan 1856 C.S. Stribling

White Bull Taken by Geo.W. Brown 5 miles from New Liberty near Browns Mill on Twin Creek appraised by Elisha Arnold 2 feb 1856 J.M. Coates

Red Steer Taken by Agnes J. Green 4 miles from New Liberty on Eagle Creek appraised by James Gayle

p232

R & W Heifer Taken by Saml. B. Morehead on Frankfort road near Franklin County line 5 miles from Monterey 1 nov 1856 (by police Judge) Jas. Fitzgerrald

Red Steer Taken by Wm. Glass 7 nov 1856 F.L. Glass

Bay Mare Taken by John Brock Sr. near Popular Grove 27 oct 1855   J.J. Stewart

p233

Bay Mare Taken by William Thornberry on Frankfort Road 3 miles from Owenton 25 jun 1856   C.S. Stribling

Bay Mare Taken by D.H. Morgan near Mascedonia Church 1 oct 1856   J.J. Stewart

Roan Heifer Taken by James S. Minor on road to Sanders Old Mill 3 miles from New Liberty   9 jun 1855

p234

Six Hogs — Taken by Hazelwood Moore 4 miles from New Liberty on the road to Ghent at the ford on Eagle Creek appraised by James S. Minor   1 feb 1855   J.M. Coates

Six Sheep — Taken by Hiram Stamper near Pleasant Ridge Meeting House appraised by D. L. Bryan   13 feb 1854   Jno. S. Snape

Spotted Sow — Taken by Benjamin Searcey near Popular Grove 18 feb 1854 J.J. Stewart

p235

Roan Steer — Taken by W. A. Branham near Eagle Creek and the mouth of Buck Run 18 oct 1855 W.D. Alexander

Red Cow — Taken by Lewis L. Noel in NE corner of county near Castlemans Mill on Eagle Creek   25 nov 1856 J.J. Stewart

Grey Filly — Taken by Tobias Wilhoite 12 jun 1856   James Fitzerrald

p236

White Steer — Taken by James Snelson appraised by C.H. Duvall and W.T. Suter   25 dec 1856 C.S. Stribling

R & W Steer — Taken by William Fowles near Tobias Wilhoite's Mill and 3 miles from Monterey 27 nov 1856 Jas. Fitzgerrald

p237

Red Heifer — Taken by William Fowles living near Tobias Wilhoite's Mill 2 1/2 to 3 miles from Monterey 27 nov 1856 Jas. Fitzgerrald

Pided Heifer — Taken by Samuel B. Morehead on Frankfort road near county line and 5 miles from Monterey 1 nov 1856 Jas. Fitzgerrald

Roan Heifer — Taken by Richard Sebree 6 miles E of Monterey 10 dec 1856 Jas. Fitzgerrald

p238

Black Heifer — Taken by John W. Smith near Monterey 16 jan 1857 Jas. Fitzgerrald

Heifer Calf — Taken by John G. Slaughter near Sparta appraised by Wm. (Snirvin) 28 feb 1858 J.M. Reeds

Small   Taken by W. J. Ford 4 miles N of Owenton
Filly   20 mar 1858   Wm. Cobb

p239
Bay   Taken by Barnett Noel near Popular Grove
Mare   17 sep 1857   John Cannon

Bay   Taken by B.F. True out Beech Branch Road 2 miles E of
Filly   Lusby's Mill 26 jul 1858   Jesse Holbrook

Eight   Taken by John B. McHatton on Hunters Mill Road 3 1/2 miles
Hogs   W of Owenton 20 sep 18--   Wm. Cobb

p240
Sorrel   Taken by David Wilhoite
Mare   29 nov 1858 W.B. Roberts

Red   Taken by S. P. Duvall 2 1/2 miles W of Owenton appraised by
Steer   Widow Sleet and ( ) McHatton 31 dec 1858 Wm. McHatton

p241
R & W   Taken by Lewis Roland 2 1/2 miles from Owenton on Lusby Mill
Heifer   Road 20 dec 1858 Wm. McHatton

White   Taken by Nancy S. Ford on the Owenton to New Liberty road
Heifer   appraised by John S. Ford & H.C. Ford
             18 jan 1859 Wm. McHatton

p242
Brindle   Taken by Tobias Wilhoite
Steer   26 nov 1858   S.B. Calvert

Red   Taken by Wm. Bond at Sparta on Eagle Creek
Heifer   12 feb 1858 Jas. M. Reed

White   Taken by Joel T. Garvey on the road from Caleb Jones to Warsaw
Bull   near Samuel Green's on Eagle Creek appraised by John Slaughter

p243
Bull   Taken by Norvill Wilhoite 5 1/2 miles SE of Owenton on Severn
Calf   Creek appraised by J.B. Hancock and Oliver Wilhoite
             3 jan 1859 Wm. McHatton

Roan Steer — Taken by J.B. McHatton 3/4 mile E of Owenton on road to Hunter's Mill appraised by W. Sleet & George Dean 9 nov 1859   M. Dawson

p244
Red Heifer — Taken by W. J. Ford on the road from Owenton to New Liberty 23 nov 1859   Ed. Lusby

Red Steer — Taken by Mary Ford about 3 miles N of Owenton appraised by W.J. Ford 25 nov 1859 Ed. Lusby

p245
Red Heifer — Taken by Richard Osburn 3 miles SE of Owenton appraised by W.D. Beck & Sandford Foster 25 nov 1859 Ed. Lusby

Spotted Heifer — Taken by W. J. Hughs on Main Eagle Creek one mile from Reynolds (Mins) , W & one mile from Campbell's Mills on Cobbs Station Road at the saw mills appraised by S. A. Hudson 26 nov 1859 A. Hughs

p246
Cattle Bull — Taken by Henry Morgan 4 miles W of New Liberty on Twin Creek   31 dec 1859   J.M. Coates

Red Steer — Taken by William R. (Eunes) on farm at old steam mill on Brush Creek 9 jan 1860 John Cannon

p247
Bay Horse — Taken by John W. Ogden 3 1/2 miles from New Liberty on the Marion Road 7 may 1860 M. Dawson

Bay Horse — Taken by Joseph Perry on Brush Creek 2 miles NE of Popular Grove   12 may 1860   John Cannon

p248
Sorrel Horse — Taken by R. Munday appraised by N.C. Cook and Thos. P. Herndon   22 jun 1860 Ed. Lusby

Sorrel Mare — Taken by Columbus C. Adkins 1 mile from Popular Grove 29 aug 1860   John Cannon

p249
R & W Heifer — Taken by John Holbert 5 miles E of Owenton on Campbell's Mill road appraised by L.H. Vall 4 dec 1860 Ed. Lusby

Red   Taken by W.J. Hughes 1 mile SE of Campbell's Mill on Main
Heifer   Eagle Creek on Cobb's Station Road 26 nov 1859 S. Hughes

p250
Red   Taken by L. Lewis 1 mile E of New Columbus
Heifer   appraised by J.A. eob Lzrus 25 oct 1860 O. Hughes

Sorrel   Taken by Columbus Adkins 1 mile from Popular Grove
Mare   29 aug 1860 John Cannon

p251
Spotted   Taken by H.J. Glass 1 mile N of New Columbus S of G.S. Lewis
Steer   farm on 1 aug 1861 appraised by John A. Wilson
            1 nov 1861 O. Hughes

White   Taken by G. W. Brumback 6 miles NE of Owenton appraised
Steer   by A. Caldwell 18 nov 1861 Ed Lusby

p252
R & W   Taken by Jasper N. Beck 3 miles SE of Owenton appraised
Steer   by J.H. Kelly and F. M. Beck 19 nov 1861 Ed Lusby

Bay   Taken by William Glass 1/2 mile W of Malloy's Mill
Horse   1 feb 1862 O.Hughes

Red   Taken by N.W. (Seer) 1 1/2 mile W of Smith's Mill on Eagle
Cow   Creek   appraised by James M. Taylor 5 feb 1862 O.Hughes

p253
Dark   Taken by Jesse Holbrook 1/2 mile S of Lusby's Mill
Mare   25 jun 1862 Hugh Stamper

Roan   Taken by Lewis Vallandingham 5 miles S of Lusby's Mill
Mare   16 aug 1863 Hugh Stamper

p254
Two   Taken by J. M. Beck 3 miles SE of Owenton appraised by
Steers   Richard & Tarlton Smith -Sat- Ed Lusby

R & W   Taken by Alexander Wilson 5 miles NW of Harmony near
Heifer   the road from Owenton to the Stamping Ground near
            Maj. Ben Haydon's appraised by George Marshall &
            T.H. Coleman 1 jan 1863 A.J. (Morel)

p255
Red   Taken by George Marshall 5 miles NW of Harmony on the
Steer   N side of the Owenton/Stamping Ground road near Maj. Ben
             Haydon's appraised by A.M. Wilson & Thos. H. Coleman
             16 jan 1863 A. J. (Morel)

p256
Sorrell Taken by J.W. Wilhoite 5 miles SE of Owenton
Mare   apr 1863   Ed Lusby

R & W   Taken by B.J.H. Smith and posted by P.H. Smith appraised
Steer   by J.W. Thornton & W. B. Duvall 15 nov 1863 Ed Lusby

These entries are on unnumbered pages following the above and they
  appear to be original slips of paper from Justices attached to book.

p257
Sorrel   Taken by David Wilhoite
Mare   29 nov 1858 Wm. B. Roberts

p258
Brindle Taken by Tobias Wilhoite
Steer   26 nov 1858 S. B. Calvert

Bay   Taken by B.F. Reed 2 miles E of Lusby's Mills on the Beech
Mare   Branch road   26 jul 1858 Jesse Holbrook

p259
Black   Taken by W.D. Beck appraised by W.W. Ballard & T. A. King
Sow   17 jan 1859 W. M. Hallon

Bay   Taken by John W. Odgen 3 1/2 miles from New Liberty on road
Horse   to Marion 7 may 1860 M. Dawson

Bay   Taken by Joseph Denny on Brush Creek 2 miles NE of Popular
Horse   Grove 12 may 1860 John Cannon

p260
Eight   Taken by John B. McHatton 3 1/2 miles W of Owenton on the
Hogs   Hunter Mill road appraised by W. Sleet & James Wigington
             20 sep 1858   Wm. McHatton

Black   Taken by John (W---)(torn) at Monterey
Heifer   16 jan 1857 Jas. Fitzgerrald

p261

R & W
Heifer Taken by Alexander Wilson 5 miles NW of Harmony near the
Owenton/Stamping Ground road & Maj. Ben Haydon's
appraised by George Marshall & T.W. Coleman
1 jan 1863 A.D. Moreland

p262

Roan
Steer Taken by S.P. Duvall 2 1/2 miles W of Owenton on the Pore
House Farm appraised by Headin Sleet & J.B. McHatton
3 dec 1858 Wm. McHatton

Redd
Steer Taken by William R. Emry on Brush Creek
9 jan 1860 John Cannon

R & W
Steer Taken by Jasper N. Beck 3 miles SE of Owenton
9 nov 1861 Ed Lusby

p263

Red
Heifer Taken by G.L. Lewis 1 mile N of New Columbus appraised by
Jacob Lynn   25 oct 1860 O. Hughes

R & W
Steer Taken by John Holbert 5 miles E of Owenton on the Campbell's
Mill road appraised by L. H. Vallandingham
4 dec 1860 Ed Lusby

p264

Horse (Badly torn) Taken by N.W. Lee 1 1/2 miles W on Main Eagle
Creek appraised by Jas. M. Taylor feb 1862 O.Hughes

Sorrel
Mare Taken by Columbus C. Adkins 1 mile from Popular Grove
29 aug 1860 John Cannon

p265

Bay
Mare Taken by Barnet Noel near Popular Grove
14 sep 1857 John Cannon

Read
Heifer Taken by W. J. Hughes on Main Eagle Creek 1 mile W of
Runnoldses Mill 1 mile SE of Campbell's Mill on Cobb's
Station road appraised by S.A. Hudson 26 nov 1859 O. Hughes

p266

Read
Steer Taken by George Marshall on his property 5 miles NW of
Harmony N side of the Owenton/Stamping Ground road near
Maj. Ben Haydon's appraised by A.M. Wilson & Thomas W.
Coleman   16 jan 1863 A.D. Moreland

Red Steer — Taken by Henry Morgan 4 miles W of New Liberty on Twin Creek appraised by W.H. Ligon 31 dec 1859 (J.M. Coates)

p267 Sorrel Mare — Taken by J.W. Wilhoite 5 miles SE of Owenton 2 par 1863 Ed. Lusby

White Steer — Taken by G.W. Brumback 6 miles NE of Owenton appraised by A. Caldwell 18 nov 1861 Ed. Lusby

p268 Heifer Calf — Taken by John G. Slaughter near Sparta appraised by William (Skirvin) 28 feb 1857 Jas. M. Reeds

Small Filly — Taken by W.G. Ford 4 miles N of Owenton 20 mar 1858 Wm. Cobb

p269 Three Hoggs — Taken by Robert Low near the steam mill on Brush Creek appraised by John Conover 6 mar 1857 Jas. M. Reeds

Steere — Taken by Jeremiah Garvey on the turnpike 2 miles from Ross Mill appraised by Charles Slaughter Jr. 7 --- 1857 Jas. M. Reeds

p270 White Calf — Taken by Lewis G. Noel near Castleman's Mill on Eagle Creek 10 jan 1859 John Cannon

Too Steers — Taken by J.N. Beck about 3 miles SE of Owenton appraised by Richard & Taltarn Smith -- Ed. Lusby

p271 Sorrel Horse — Taken by Dancel Smoot 8 miles from Owenton appraised by Joshua Wilhoite & Wm.W. Locke Joel Herndon

Bay Horse — Taken by William (----   --) 1/2 mile from Mallory's Mill feb 1862 O. (Hughes)

p272 Steer — Taken by Robert Bond at Sparta on Eagle Creek appraised by William Bond 20 nov 1857 Jas. M. Reeds

END — No. 3 Martha & 2 children & Garrison valued $1500, Rose $425 and Jno. G. Roberts to pay 166.66

Entry page 130

Sorrel Horse & Roan Horse

Taken up by John Stonestreet living in Owen County about 6 miles from Owenton near the road to Clay's Lick two horse beasts of the following description towit a sorrell horse 10 to 11 year old both hind feet white small blaze in his face no marks or brands perceivable 15 hands and once inch high appraised to $35 also a roan horse five years old about 14 1/2 hands high black main tail and legs no marks or brands perceivable appraised to $30 before me the 22nd day of Sept 1832

Entry page 249

Red Heifer

Taken up as a stray by W. J. Hughes in the county of Owen on the waters of Main Eagle Creek one mile from Campbells Mill southeast of said mill on the Cobbs Station road from said mills a red yearling heifer no ear marks star in the forehead white stripe on the left shoulder and white pides on the right & left flanks taken the 10th day of October and appraised at six dollars by S. A. Hudson the same having been sworn by me Given under my hand Nov 26 1859 O. Hughes JPOC

My number one rule is :
"Don't abstract records with unfamiliar names."

I am guilty of breaking that rule, but I feel these records provide valuable site information and anyone with Owen County ancestors will be able to determine the correct names.

Although I have some family from Owen County there are several names here which are unfamiliar and the clerk's hand writing is often undecipherable.

Originally, I was trying to get proof of a Hoover family connection. I did find that family, but I also discovered roots for oddly named uncles Sebree and Calvert.

All records are valuable, if you take the time to study them.

Poor Handwriting and Odd Spellings
(may be another spelling or it may not)
some obvious - some weird

Absher = Absted = Abston = Abches   (some Abstons close by)

Branham = Branaham = Brinham

Brombley = Brmble

Bendles = Brindle

Brown = Bowen (both ??) (Are they all Brown)

Brown or Bowen = Bonm = Bowne = Bowsn

Claxon = Claxton

Dews = Devi

Dixon = Down

Walter Garrett = Waller = Wauler = Miller

Guill = Quill

LDvngan ???

Jemmerson = Linerson

Litzland = Fitzgerald

Monday = Munday

Mothe (torn) = Mothershead

Redden = Redding

Skirvin = Snirvin (Your guess is as good as mine ??)

Spears = Speirs = Spires

TAbram ---   Thnkald ----   ????????

(--), John, 17
  Thomas, 12
(--ton), Luke, 15
-, Garrison, 41
  Martha & 2 ch, 41
Abbott, W.R., 24
Absher, John, 07
Absted, John, 03
Abston, John, 14
Achbes, John, 08
Adkins, Columbus, 38
  Columbus C., 37, 40
  James, 29
  Walter, 02
Alexander, Angus, 04
  W.D., 35
Allsmith, G.W., 21
Alte, S., 21
Altzman, Moses, 34
Arnold, Elisha, 34
Aserwall, T., 21
Ayers, Lewis, 02, 26, 32
  S.R., 34
Bacon, J.C., 04
  Jno.C., 16
  John C., 04
  Jon C., 10
  N.M., 04, 05, 06, 07,
    08, 09, 10, 11, 12,
    14, 15, 16, 17
Bainbridge, E., 31
Baininap, C., 27
Baker, John J., 24
  John T., 07
  Joseph, 34
  Saml.J., 18
Ballard, John, 10
  Johnson, 01
  W.S., 01
  W.W., 39
  Whit, 17
Banks, S.D., 01
Barker, Jesse, 22
Barns, William, 01
Barr, William, 07, 12
Bates, George Sr., 33
  Willis, 11, 28
Beck, F.M., 38
  J.N., 41

Jasper N., 38, 40
  W.D., 37, 39
Bendles, John, 26
Berryman, Thomas A., 02,
    20
  Thos.A., 34
Bibb, Daniel, 16
Bishop, John, 02
Bohannon, H.D., 10
Bond, Robert, 41
  Samuel S., 18, 31
  William, 41
  Wm., 36
Bonds, Robert, 22
Bonm, John, 26
Bowen, John, 14, 28
  William, 14
Bowen, John, 31
Bowsn, Wm., 32
Bradney, A., 22
Bramblett, William, 04
Branaham, G.C., 17
Branham, G.C., 14, 09,
    10, 11, 12, 15, 16,
    17, 19, 20, 23, 24,
    25, 26, 27
  W.A., 35
Brindle, John, 29
Brinham, G.C., 08, 09
Briscoe, M.D., 30
Briscol, Lindsey, 28
Brmble, Thomas, 20
Brock, James, 03
  Jas., 19
  John, 32
  John Sr., 34
Bromley, Thomas, 09
Brown, F., 27, 29, 31, 33
  Geo.W., 34
  Isaac, 19
  John, 01, 03, 04, 05,
    07, 09, 12, 13,
    14(2), 16, 17, 18,
    27, 31
  Thomas, 23, 31
  Thos., 22
  William, 14
  Wm., 20, 28, 29
Brumback, G.W., 38, 41
Brumfield, Mens, 12

6

OWNE COUNTY STRAY 2

Bryan, D.L., 35
Burk, Mason, 30
  Robt., 23
Burns, M., 17
Caldwell, A., 41
  Joseph, 12, 25
Calvert, Henry, 21
  James H., 21
  John B., 15
  S., 02, 11, 12, 13,
    18, 19
  S.B., 26, 36, 39
Cannon, John, 36, 37, 38,
    39, 40, 41
Carlten, James, 31
Carlton, James, 03
Carter, Henry S., 01
  Spencer, 28
  Thomas, 09, 10, 11,
    24, 26, 28
Castleman, John L., 31
Cathrit, J.B., 26
Catterson, W., 27
Chandler, Lydid, 25
  Uriah, 02, 04, 06, 21
Clark, Absolum, 08
  Harvey, 09
  Henry, 10
  J.M., 34
  Jn., 27
  John W., 27
  Robt. (colored), 14
Clarke, Absolum, 18
  Henry, 09, 18
Claxon, C., 01, 07, 09,
    10, 11, 25
  Chaus, 22
  David, 31
  James, 09, 24
Claxton, C., 03, 05, 08
  Calistine, 08
  Classius, 05
Clifton, Charles, 17, 29
Clinn, Morgan B., 26
Coates, J.M., 35, 37, 41
  Willis, 29
Coats, J.M., 33
Cobb, Asa, 23, 25, 27,
    28, 29
  E., 02, 07, 08, 09, 14

Elisha, 04, 05
  William, 02, 36, 41
Coleman, T.H., 38
  T.W., 40
  Thomas W., 40
  Thos.H., 39
Conder, David, 32
Conn, Diana, 01
Conover, John, 41
Cooper, J.E., 33
Covington, Luke, 17
Crable, David, 08
Crawford, William, 18
Crouch, Reuben, 05
Cumble, Thos., 18
Curry, Elijah C., 26
  William Sr., 17
Davidson, James, 23
Davis, C.W., 23
Dawson, M., 37, 39
Dean, George, 37
Dellauder, Jessy, 13
Denny, Joseph, 39
Devi, John H., 16
Devon, Dicy, 05
Dews, John H., 12, 14
Dillon, Thomas B., 04
Dixon, Moses, 08
Down, Moses, 11
Duvall, C.H., 35
  Charles, 17
  Francis A., 17
  James F., 26
  Jonas, 08
  R.M., 04
  S.P., 36, 40
  W.B., 39
Edwards, A.V., 31
  R.L., 29, 30, 31
Elliot, Henry, 11
Ellis, Duncan, 17
  James, 30
Emry, William R., 40
English, J.B., 21, 25
Ervin, William, 11
Eunes, William R., 37
Evans, S.D., 24
Exter, George, 30
Ferguson, J.M., 30
Fitzarel, Ellis, 10

Fitzarel, Ellis, 10
Fitzgerald, Ellis, 08
Fitzgerrald, James, 35
  Jas., 34, 39
Fitzjarrel, Ellis, 10
Fleming, L.J., 24
  L.T., 25
Flemings, Leonard J., 16
Ford, Ben, 16
  H.C., 36
  Harlin H., 26
  James, 16
  John S., 36
  Mary, 37
  Nancy S., 36
  W.G., 41
  W.J., 36, 37
Foster, Sandford, 37
Fowles, William, 35
Fulson, John T., 15
Gale, H.B., 31
  Jas. H., 03
Garnett, Walter, 19
Garret, Jemason, 22
Garrett, Granville, 21
  Miller, 29
  Waller, 33
  Wauler, 05
  William, 11, 30
Garvey, Jeremiah, 05, 30,
  41
  Joel T., 36
Garvy, J., 20, 22, 26
  John, 20
  John L., 20
  L., 19
Gayle, James, 34
Geott, Joseph, 06
Giles, H., 24, 26, 28,
  30, 31
Ginn, J.C., 27
Glass, B., 21
  Bexfield, 19, 20, 21
  F.L., 34
  H.B., 18
  H.J., 38
  J.C., 27, 30
  John, 04
  William, 20, 34, 38
Gnyon, William, 17

Grable, David, 30
Gravey, J., 18
Green, Aaron, 10
  Agnes J., 34
  Jesse L., 33
  Samuel, 36
Gregory, John, 02
  Thomas, 15, 24
Griffin, Levi, 15
Guill, W.B., 05, 15
  Wilson B., 15
Haddon, William, 05, 07,
  11
Hale, Peter, 27
Hall, M., 34
Hallon, W.M., 39
Hammons, G.W., 34
Hancock, Ambrose C., 23
  J.B., 36
  John B., 14, 22, 30
  Thomas, 12
Hanks, S.D., 02, 03, 05,
  08, 10
  Sydnor D., 03, 04
Hardin, Absalem, 24
  Thomas, 14, 15, 33
Harrison, Andrew, 18
  Wm.J., 18
Haskins, T.G., 33
Hatton, Wm., 16
Hawkins, Jos.F., 10
  Joseph F., 08
  William, 30
Hayden, Benjamin, 23
Haydon, B., 19, 27, 28,
  29, 30(2)
  Ben, 25
  Benj., 16, 17, 18
  Maj.Ben, 18, 38, 39,
  40
Hearn, Andrew, 27
  James, 19
  James A., 12
Henrdon, James, 25
Herndon, James, 07, 08
  Joel, 05, 07, 11, 20,
  27, 28, 30, 31, 41
  Thos.P., 37
Hesler, Jacob, 06, 10, 23
Hesman, Charles, 31

8

OWNE COUNTY STRAY 2

Hill, J.L., 34
    Wm.H., 32
Hiter, Adam, 08
Holaday, Benjmain, 01
Holbert, Jno., 29
    John, 37, 40
Holbrook, Colby, 03
    Jesse, 36, 38, 39
    John, 09
Holbrooks, Wil, 34
Holiman, Jacob H., 21
Holliday, Ben, 03
Hoover, David, 16
Howe, William, 04
Hudson, John B., 19
    S.A., 37, 40
Hughes, O., 38, 40, 41
    S., 38
    W.J., 38
    William Sr., 15
Hughes, W.J., 40
Hughs, A., 37
    W.J., 37
    Wm. J., 31
Huoald, H.B., 12
Ingram, John, 14
Irossion, Jacob, 12
Ivy, Absolum, 04, 05
Jackson, Hezekiah, 13
    Keer, 12
    Simeon, 04
    William, 05
Jameson, Robert A., 29
Jemmerson, George B., 25
Jennings, John, 11
Johnson, B.D., 23
    Sandford, 19, 29
    Thos., 18
Jones, Caleb, 01, 36
    John O., 21
    Jonas, 02, 05, 07, 20,
       22
    Robt., 27
    Solomon, 17
    Thomas, 16
Jordan, Thomas, 11
Kateman, Uriah, 27
Kelly, J.H., 38
Kemper, B., 22
    Charles, 12

R.J., 19
Kendall, Rowland, 30
Kenny, Jas. E., 21
Kimper, B.J., 29
King, T.A., 39
    Wm., 14
Kinnon, Dr.R., 32
Latta, Matthew, 20
Latts, Mathew, 25
LDvngan, William, 23
Lee, Jos., 17
    Jos. R., 17
    N.W., 40
Leonard, John, 10
Lewis, G.L., 40
    G.S., 38
    Hulden, 24
    L., 38
    Wm., 32
Ligon, W.H., 41
Linerson, George B., 23
Linn, William, 23
LitzLand, Ellis, 20
Locke, Wm.W., 41
Long, Brumfield, 06
    William, 03
    Wm., 04, 05
Louderback, Wm., 20
Loules, William, 27
Lovejoy, Polly, 18
Low, Robert, 41
Lowderback, John, 15
Lumer, William, 21
Lusby, Ed, 37, 38, 39,
       40, 41
    Wm., 31
Lutes, Thomas, 05
Lynn, Jacob, 40
    William, 17, 25
Lysby, John, 33
Lzrus, J.A.cob, 38
McAndrew, L., 17
McClure, J.D., 16, 17,
       19, 20
    Jno. D., 29, 30
    John D., 23
McDaniel, James C., 12
    James E., 24
    Jas.E., 13
McFenny, Jno. R., 29

McFerron, Jess, 33
  John Sr., 33
  Wm., 33
McFerson, Jno.Sr., 16
McHatton, J.B., 37, 40
  John B., 36, 39
  Lytte, 30
  William, 30
  Wm., 32(2), 33, 36,
    39, 40
McKensey, John, 18
McKensy, Thos., 19
McKinsie, John, 22
McNeal, John, 21
McPherron, Wm., 33
McSute, Wm., 04
Madda, David, 12
Maddox, Sherwood, 01
  W.M., 22
Marshall, George, 09, 21,
    38, 39, 40
Martin, Benjamin, 23
Mason, Bartlett B., 14
  Samuel, 14
  Sanderson, 25, 32
Mathers, Morris, 03
Maxwell, James, 23
May, Thomas, 33
Meek, John, 03, 10, 11
Miner, Edwind, 29
Minor, James S., 34, 35
Mins, Reynolds, 37
Molone, Alfred, 18
Monday, Harrison, 02
Montgomery, Wm., 26
Moore, Alexander, 23
  Frances, 22
  Hazelwood, 35
  John, 01
Morehead, Saml.B., 34
  Samuel B., 35
Morel, A.J., 38, 39
Moreland, A.D., 40
Morgan, D.H., 34
  Henry, 37, 41
  Lewis, 23
Mothe, Alvan, 04
Mothershead, A., 32
  Alvan, 20
Munday, Harrison, 03

Hearlison, 23
  R., 37
Munston, Wm., 15
Murphy, -, 24
Murray, John, 03
Musselman, Jacob, 30
Musvey, Jno. B., 31
Neal, Wm.E., 26
Noel, Barret, 30
  Barrett, 36
  Lewis G., 41
  Lewis L., 35
  R.S., 31
O'Banion, Bryan, 05
Odgen, John W., 39
Ogden, John W., 37
Oliver, Willis, 26
O'Neal, Jas., 19
Orr, James P., 31
Osburn, Richard, 37
  Richardson A., 02
Parker, John, 06
Perkin, Jeremiah, 28
Perkins, William, 07
Perry, George, 19
  Joseph, 07, 37
Poe, Edmund, 26
Pryor, James, 22
Quill, H.B., 03
  W.B., 11
Quisenberry, John, 20
Ransdell, W.C., 32
Razor, George, 08
  Jacob, 33
  Joseph, 33
Ream, T.H., 24
Redden, John, 15
Redding, John, 06
Reed, B.F., 39
  Jas.M., 36
Reeds, J.M., 35
  Jas.M., 41
Revill, R.R., 30, 31
Rey--, Alexander, 09
Richardson, William, 01
Riddle, John, 21
Rigg, Douglass, 11
Ritchey, Ezekiel, 03
  Thos.A., 22
  Thos.H., 23, 24

R. Smith 25

W.H., 20
William, 01
Smoot, Dancel, 41
  Patsy, 28
Snape, J.S., 32
  Jno.S., 32, 33, 34, 35
Snelson, James, 35
Snirvin, Wm., 35
Song, Bromfield, 10
Sonles, Oliver, 08
Southoite, Charles, 10
Sparks, A.J., 15
  John, 10
  Maddison, 10
  Mullison, 09
Spears, John, 04
Speirs, John, 12
Spires, Jeremiah, 06
  John, 09(2), 10
  Lucy, 09
Squires, R.F., 23
  R.T., 27
Stackhouse, Dr.John, 32
Stamper, H.S., 33
  Hiram, 14, 35
  Hugh, 33, 38
  Jesse, 05
  Joshua, 25
Stephens, Benj., 17
Stevens, Benjamin, 23
Steward, Richard, 32
  Richard Jr., 32
Stewart, Daniel, 03
  Elijah, 18
  J.J., 34, 35
Stiger, Samuel, 22
Stonestreet, John, 07
Street, John, 12
Stribling, C.S., 34, 35
Suter, Jesse, 24
  John H., 26
  Thomas, 11
  W.T., 35
  Wm.M, 28
Syrus, Denis, 10
TAbram, W., 27
Taylor, James M., 38
  Jas.M., 40
  Smith, 29
  William, 02

Teal, William, 23
Thnkald, Gabriel, 27
Thomas, John, 22, 30
  Joseph, 21
  Joseph M., 06
  Reuben L., 33
  Rial, 26
  Robert, 03, 28
  William, 15, 22
Thornberry, William, 34
Thornton, J.W., 39
  Phillip, 28
Throbald, James F., 16
Todd, P.H., 31
  Paschal, 04
  R.H., 21
  Samuel, 02, 12, 19,
    21, 24
Tolen, William, 09
Trobridge, William L., 31
  Wm. L., 32
True, R.F., 36
  R.G., 06, 07
  Robert G., 01, 04, 05,
    08
  Thomas, 31
Tufts, Simon, 21
Twin, Garland, 14
Vall, L.H., 37
Vallandingham, George B.,
    08, 09, 12, 15
  John, 06, 10, 11
  L.H., 40
  Lewis, 38
  Rick, 01
Veal, Lewis, 23
W--, John, 39
Walden, Edmund, 26
Walker, Delvin, 03
Walter, J.M., 31
Warring, W.C., 32
Watherton, Levin, 08
Webster, Henry, 24, 27
  Isaac, 01, 26
  Jacob, 24
Welch, Henry, 26
West, Virgil, 22
Wever, A.P., 34
Whitaker, John, 19
Whitcomb, Solomon, 30

White, George, 20
  J., 33
  L., 21
  Lewis, 17, 18, 19, 20,
    21, 22, 23, 24, 25,
    26
Wigington, James, 39
Wiginton, Peter, 20
Wilhoite, Anderson, 32
  Charles J., 11
  Charles S., 31
  David, 36, 39
  Isreal, 22
  J.A., 34
  J.S., 31
  J.W., 39, 41
  Joshua, 41
  Norvill, 36
  Obadiah, 07
  Obadiah E., 14
  Oliver, 36
  Polly, 17
  Tobias, 04, 06, 08,
    10, 20, 27, 33, 35,
    36, 39
Williams, Alexander, 23
  Charles, 9
  Jno. F., 22
  John, 25
  John F., 23
  John G., 04
  Richard, 08, 16
  S.F., 33
Willton, James, 20
Wilson, A.M., 39, 40
  Alexander, 38, 40
  Ellis, 14
  J--, 13
  James, 04, 06, 22, 24
  John, 22
  John A., 38
  Nancy, 18
Wingate, C., 06, 16, 20
  Cyrus, 08, 10, 14, 17,
    18, 20, 22
  Smith, 17
Wood, Gideon, 21
  James, 03, 30
Works, John W., 05
Wright, James, 31

Yancy, R.H., 11

www.ingramcontent.com/pod-product-compliance
Lightning Source LLC
Chambersburg PA
CBHW080338270326
41927CB00014B/3270